CONTEMPORARY WRITERS

General Editors
MALCOLM BRADBURY
and
CHRISTOPHER BIGSBY

PHILIP ROTH

PHILIP
ROTH

HERMIONE LEE

METHUEN
LONDON AND NEW YORK

6/1984
Am. Lit.

To Jenny and Steve Uglow

First published in 1982 by
Methuen & Co. Ltd
11 New Fetter Lane, London EC4P 4EE
Published in the USA by
Methuen & Co.
in association with Methuen, Inc.
733 Third Avenue, New York, NY 10017

© 1982 Hermione Lee

Typeset by Rowland Phototypesetting Ltd
Printed in Great Britain by
Richard Clay (The Chaucer Press) Ltd
Bungay, Suffolk

British Library Cataloguing in Publication Data

Lee, Hermione
Philip Roth.—(Contemporary writers)
1. Roth, Philip—Criticism and interpretation
I. Title   II. Series
813'.54   PS3568.O8552/

ISBN 0-416-32980-2

Library of Congress Cataloging in Publication Data

Lee, Hermione
Philip Roth.
(Contemporary writers)
Bibliography: p.
1. Roth, Philip – Criticism and interpretation.
I. Title.   II. Series.
PS3568.O855Z76   1982   813'.54   82-8223
ISBN 0-416-32980-2 (pbk.)

CONTENTS

GENERAL EDITORS' PREFACE

Over the past twenty years or so, it has become clear that a decisive change has taken place in the spirit and character of contemporary writing. There now exists around us, in fiction, drama and poetry, a major achievement which belongs to our experience, our doubts and uncertainties, our ways of perceiving – an achievement stylistically radical and novel, and likely to be regarded as quite as exciting, important and innovative as that of any previous period. This is a consciousness and a confidence that has grown very slowly. In the 1950s it seemed that, somewhere amidst the dark realities of the Second World War, the great modernist impulse of the early years of this century had exhausted itself, and that the post-war arts would be arts of recessiveness, pale imitation, relative sterility. Some, indeed, doubted the ability of literature to survive the experiences of holocaust. A few major figures seemed to exist, but not a style or a direction. By the 1960s the confidence was greater, the sense of an avant-garde returned, the talents multiplied, and there was a growing hunger to define the appropriate styles, tendencies and forms of a new time. And by the 1970s it was not hard to see that we were now surrounded by a remarkable, plural, innovative generation, indeed several layers of generations, whose works represented a radical inquiry into contemporary forms and required us to read and understand – or, often, to read and *not* understand – in quite new ways. Today, as the 1980s start, that cumulative post-war achievement has acquired a degree of coherence that allows for critical response and understanding; hence the present series.

We thus start it in the conviction that the age of Beckett, Borges, Nabokov, Bellow, Pynchon, Robbe-Grillet, Golding, Murdoch, Fowles, Grass, Handke and Calvino, of Albee, Mamet, Shepard, Ionesco, Orton, Pinter and Stoppard, of Ginsberg, Lowell, Ashbery, Paz, Larkin and Hughes, and many another, is indeed an outstanding age of international creation, striking experiment, and some degree of aesthetic coherence. It is a time that has been described as 'post-modern', in the sense that it is an era consequent to modernism yet different from it, having its own distinctive preoccupations and stylistic choices. That term has its limitations, because it is apt to generate too precise definitions of the contemporary experiment, and has acquired rather too specific associations with contemporary American writing; but it does help concentrate our sense of living in a distinctive period. With the new writing has come a new criticism or rather a new critical theorem, its thrust being 'structuralist' or 'deconstructive' – a theorem that not only coexists with but has affected that writing (to the point where many of the best theorists write fictions, the best fictionalists write criticism). Again, its theory can be hermetic and enclosing, if not profoundly apocalyptic; but it points to the presence in our time of a new sense of the status of word and text, author and reader, which shapes and structures the making of modern form.

The aim of 'Contemporary Writers' is to consider some of the most important figures in this scene, looking from the standpoint of and at the achievement of the writers themselves. Its aims are eclectic, and it will follow no tight definition of the contemporary; it will function on the assumption that contemporary writing is by its nature multidirectional and elusive, since styles and directions keep constantly changing in writers who, unlike the writers of the past, are continuous, incomplete, not dead (though several of these studies will address the careers of those who, though dead, remain our contemporaries, as many of those who continue to write are manifestly not). A fair criticism of living writers must be assertive but also provisional, just as a fair sense of contemporary style must be open to that most crucial of contemporary awarenesses, that of the suddenness of change. We do not assume, then, that there is one right path to contemporary experiment, nor that a self-conscious reflexiveness, a deconstructive strategy, an art of performance or a metafictional mode is the only one of current importance. As Iris Murdoch said, 'a strong agile realism which is of course not photographic naturalism' – associated perhaps especially with British writing, but also with Latin-American and American – is also a major component of modern style.

So in this series we wish to identify major writers, some of whom are avant-garde, others who are familiar, even popular, but all of whom are in some serious sense contemporary and in some contemporary sense serious. The aim is to offer brief, lucid studies of their work which draw on modern theoretical issues but respond, as much modern criticism does not, to their distinctiveness and individual interest. We have looked for contributors who are engaged with their subjects – some of them being significant practising authors themselves, writing out of creative experience, others of whom are critics whose interest is personal as well as theoretical. Each volume will provide a thorough account of the author's work so far, a solid bibliography, a personal judgement – and, we hope, an enlarged understanding of writers who are important, not only because of the individual force of their work, but because they are ours in ways no past writer could really be.

Norwich, England, 1981   MALCOLM BRADBURY
                                            CHRISTOPHER BIGSBY

PREFACE AND ACKNOWLEDGEMENTS

At the end of the 1950s a brilliant, youthful collection of sharply observed stories about Jews in America won the National Book Award and aroused furious hostility among conservative Jewish readers. A decade later, the author of these stories became internationally notorious with the outrageous 'confessions' of a Jewish son with sexual problems. Ten years after that, at the end of the seventies, he produced two elegant fictionalized histories of a successful Jewish-American writer's dilemmas in the sixties and seventies. (There is soon to be a third in this series.) Now that he is no longer the *enfant terrible* of American-Jewish fiction, but a highly respected novelist in his middle years, it is possible to take stock of Philip Roth's achievement – of the range and quality of his work, and of his status as a 'contemporary writer'.

Philip Roth made a late entry into the Jewish-American cultural tradition of the forties and fifties, a tradition dominated by moral seriousness, responsible aspirations towards self-fulfilment in an alien or brutal Gentile world, and formal narrative constraints. His earlier work shared these conscientious qualities with, for example, Bernard Malamud's *The Assistant* (1957), Saul Bellow's *The Adventures of Augie March* (1953) and Lionel Trilling's literary essays (such as 'Manners, Morals and the Novel', delivered in 1947 and published in *The Liberal Imagination* in 1950). But, from the start, there were also signs of a savage playfulness which looked back to the black surrealism of Nathanael West in the

Depression years, and forward to Lennie Bruce's desperate joking in the sixties. These signs prefigured Roth's breaking out, with *Portnoy's Complaint*, as the 'bad boy' of Jewish-American letters: part of a break-out and break-down (what Roth calls a 'demythologizing' process) through all of American politics and society and literature. The subversion of old faiths and sanctions, in which Roth played a very important part, entailed a laying waste of literary proscriptions. Like other 'key' American fictions of the demythologizing era (*Couples*, *Last Exit to Brooklyn*, *The Group*, *V.*, *The Naked Lunch*), Roth's fiction made 'unexpurgated' use of post-Korean America's most painful concerns. Psychoanalysis, alienation, erotic fixations, pornography, urban violence, strains on the family, divorce, anxiety about eastern Europe, alarm at the implications of Zionism for twentieth-century Jewish history, dismay at the ineffectuality of liberalism, and national political guilt and disillusion, were appropriated by Roth, and by other writers, as raw material.

The registering of contemporary American subject-matter involved a radical reworking of fictional forms. Roth's development has been threefold. He moved from the 'nets' of the Jewish cultural ghetto to wider, if alien, world spaces (while continuing to write about American Jews). He grew up, with the rest of America, from the relative innocence of the fifties to the scepticism of the eighties. His fictional strategies changed from anecdotal realism to making play with surrealism, pastiche, confessionals, case-histories and psychic fantasies (the narrative as *mouth*), and, most recently, to coolly objectified 'autobiographies'.

In the whole spread of Roth's work so far, we can find a sensationally energetic and stylish reflection of, and response to, the American experience of the last three decades. In detail, we find in each book an idiosyncratic (and self-aware) mixture of literary allegiances: to a Jamesian or Flaubertian high artistic seriousness; to an eastern European tradition, a fiction of proscription and blockage derived from Kafka and Gogol; and to the self-punishing wisecracks of the Jewish clown. Roth's stylistic and emotional range, and his commitment to

10

the real world he lives in, makes him, as I hope to show, one of the most significant and remarkable of contemporary writers: bold, cunning, humane, ambitious, versatile and wise.

My thanks go to the University of York for a sabbatical term during which this book was written, and, for help and advice of various kinds, to Philip French, Matthew Hoffman, Dinos Patrides, Alistair Stead and, above all, John Barnard. I am grateful to Judith Bates for typing the manuscript.

The author and publisher would like to thank the following for permission to reproduce copyright material: Farrar, Straus & Giroux, Inc. and Jonathan Cape Ltd for extracts from *Reading Myself and Others*.

University of York, 1982   HERMIONE LEE

A NOTE ON THE TEXTS

Not all of Philip Roth's books are available in paperback in this country. Where possible, I refer to the most easily obtainable editions. Quotations are taken from the Penguin editions of *When She Was Good*, *The Great American Novel* and *The Ghost Writer*; from the Corgi editions of *Goodbye, Columbus*, *Letting Go*, *My Life as a Man*, *Portnoy's Complaint*, *The Professor of Desire* and *Reading Myself and Others*; from the Cape edition of *Our Gang* and *Zuckerman Unbound*, and from the revised versions of 'Novotny's Pain' and *The Breast* in the Cape *Philip Roth Reader*.

The chronology of Philip Roth's major works, and the abbreviations used in this book, are as follows:

Goodbye, Columbus	1959	GC
Letting Go	1962	LG
When She Was Good	1967	WSWG
Portnoy's Complaint	1969	PC
Our Gang	1971	OG
The Breast	1972, revised 1980	B
The Great American Novel	1973	GAN
My Life as a Man	1974	MLAM
Reading Myself and Others	1975	RMAO
The Professor of Desire	1977	PD
The Ghost Writer	1979	GW
A Philip Roth Reader	1980	PRR
Zuckerman Unbound	1981	ZU

1

'ARE YOU FINISHED?'

Say 'Philip Roth', and the first reaction is likely to be a half-amused, half-queasy smile and a joking remark (possibly in a 'comic' Jewish accent) about never wanting to eat liver again. Alexander Portnoy's desecration of his own family's dinner ('my first piece I had in the privacy of my own home, rolled round my cock in the bathroom at three-thirty – and then had again on the end of a fork at five-thirty, along with the other members of that poor innocent family of mine' (*PC*, p. 150)) made Roth famous and rich, and is still his most notorious invention. But *Portnoy's Complaint* was published in 1969, and is one of eleven novels and novellas. Some of Roth's subjects since then – a man who turns into a breast, a baseball team of zombies, midgets and cripples, President 'Tricky Dixon' drowned naked in a plastic bag – might be thought quite as sensational or tasteless as the teenage Portnoy's desperate attempts at taboo-breaking, even though they never drew quite as much outraged attention. Nor is the voice of Portnoy Philip Roth's only voice. Unlike those twentieth-century American novelists whose voice *is*, unchangingly, their fiction (Kerouac, Vonnegut, Brautigan), Roth is a much more various writer than *Portnoy* on its own would suggest. But, as in his most recent novel *Zuckerman Unbound* (1981), in which the paranoid novelist Zuckerman finds himself inextricably identified with his own exhibitionist Jewish hero Carnovsky, *Portnoy* has to some extent trapped Philip Roth. Whatever else he may write, it will probably never finish being his most famous, or infamous, novel.

And, whatever else Roth deserves, that first reaction, the amused grimace of distaste, is not entirely inappropriate. It is right to associate Roth with both taste and distastefulness. Much of his comedy is (like Portnoy himself, only more successfully) taboo-breaking. Part of Roth wants to be as 'tasteless' as possible, though he is at the same time a stylish, cultured writer (and teacher) much indebted to the most tasteful of literary mentors. His novels are full of tasting and eating, licking and chewing, vomiting, regurgitating, weeping and excreting, and, conversely, of forbidden foods, constipated fathers, teachers with migraines, and women who prefer not to suck cocks or drink sperm. Roth is, pre-eminently, the novelist of orifices and blockages, of frustrated gratification.

Eating and sex, it has been observed, are parallel activities in *Portnoy's Complaint*.[1] Alex 'fucking his own family's dinner' is the most gorge-raising of a number of episodes which equate food taboos and sexual taboos. The joke of the Jewish mother with her obsessively cleaned kitchen, well-stocked fridge and horror of non-kosher food 'ain't no joke'. Mrs Portnoy's way of *shtupping* her 7-year-old son full of food is to sit over him with a breadknife when he refuses to eat; the hours he spends, as a teenager, locked in the bathroom, she attributes to his stuffing himself with 'french fries and ketchup'. 'Tell me, please, what other kind of garbage you're putting into your mouth so we can get to the bottom of this diarrhea!' (*PC*, p. 25). In the kitchen, while she is 'salting the meat so as to rid it of its blood', her own blood starts to drip, to the horror of 4-year-old Alex; years later, when he is 11, she sends him out to buy her sanitary towels. He is not allowed to eat with the *shvartze* (black) cleaning lady, or to taste lobster, which mother associates with sexual temptation. So Portnoy whacks off on the 107 bus from New York to New Jersey, just after eating his first lobster: 'That taboo so easily and simply broken, confidence may have been given to the whole slimy, suicidal Dionysian side of my nature' (*PC*, p. 87). The kosher laws say that goys will eat *anything* and, by analogy, '*will do anything as well*' (*PC*, p. 90).

Kitchen and bathroom are the crucial places in the Portnoy

household: 'the central obsession with the body' is rooted, as Roth has said, 'in the utterly mundane family setting' (*RMAO*, p. 6). While mother bleeds the meat and holds the knife, son and father compete for time on the lavatory to shed their heavy loads: 'Can I have a little peace, please, so I can get something accomplished in here?' (*PC*, p. 24).[2] Portnoy's pursuit of *shiksas* is a pursuit of 'junk' sex, unkosher goods. What he wants is freely to consume ('Did I eat!' he says of his first encounter with the Monkey) and be consumed. At the end of the book he is kicked and called pig by an Israeli girl (his mother in disguise), whose disgust at his uncleanness prompts some Portnovian bravado: 'Maybe that's all I really am, a lapper of cunts, the slavish mouth for some woman's hole. Eat! And so be it! Maybe the wisest solution is for me to live on all fours!' (*PC*, p. 305). But a bestial revelling in uncleanness isn't possible for Portnoy: he is made a man, as well as unmanned by, guilt and shame.

Eating and sex dominate this novel (as subject-matter and as metaphors); but the same concentration on consumption is found in all the other books. One of Roth's earliest comic scenes is Aunt Gladys's supervision of Neil Klugman's Newark evening meals in his first novella, 'Goodbye, Columbus' (1959). ('You're going to pick the peas out is all? You tell me that, I wouldn't buy with the carrots' (*GC*, p. 4).) Aunt Gladys's anxious clearing-out of her supplies is set against the glut of exotic fruits in the rich Patimkins' fridge, and Neil's unease at the Patimkins' wasteful materialism emerges in his account of their dinner-table conversation, 'the sentences lost in the passing of food, the words gurgled into mouthfuls, the syntax chopped and forgotten in heapings, spillings, and gorgings' (*GC*, p. 15). In *The Professor of Desire* (1977), the dying mother expresses her feelings for her son by filling up the freezer compartment of his fridge; at her funeral, the father insists on his taking 'the food she had frozen for me only the month before, the last things cooked by her on this earth' (*PD*, p. 93). Eating can be threat, promise, blackmail, prevention or protection. Zuckerman, the novelist Tarnopol's fictional self in *My Life as a Man* (1974), remembers his childhood as 'Sunday

15

sweets and sauces . . . breasts and laps' (*MLAM*, p. 77). Beastly eating lets loose the id: Baumgarten, the 'tasteless' erotomaniac poet in *The Professor of Desire*, dismisses Jewish family life with the words 'All that loving; all that hating; all those meals' (*PD*, p. 110), and tears at his food like an animal – or a cannibal. Cooking and the cooked are identified with ethics, restraint and responsible Jewishness. The mothers who impose the taboos are cooks, and so are the 'good', dutiful mistresses who make delicious meals but won't drink sperm. Savage, unmanning women break the taboos: Maureen Tarnopol, in her final showdown with her husband in *My Life as a Man*, covers his room, and is covered, with blood, tears and shit ('I gagged and averted my head' (*MLAM*, p. 288)). Lydia, her counterpart in one of Peter Tarnopol's 'Useful Fictions' within the novel, proves her madness by placing in front of herself for breakfast 'a bowl full of kitty litter, covered with urine and a sliced candle' (*MLAM*, p. 42).

Eating and excreting provide analogues not only for sexual taboo-breaking but also for the process of analysis and narrative. Mrs Portnoy's intention to 'get to the bottom of this diarrhea' might as well be Dr Spielvogel's, when faced with Portnoy's frantic logorrhoea. In *My Life as a Man*, Spielvogel, again the analyst, watches Tarnopol weep for five minutes, then asks 'Are you finished?' – as a mother might ask her child, either when it's at table or on the lavatory. Tarnopol's and Portnoy's narrative outpourings are a painful 'letting go', the only alternative to a blocked silence.

Tony Tanner, in *City of Words*, takes 'letting go' (the title, of course, of Roth's first full-length novel (1962)) as the central metaphor for mid-twentieth-century American fiction. Characters are caught between 'the dread of utter formlessness' and 'an imprisoning deathly constriction'; they are for ever trying (usually unsatisfactorily) simultaneously to let go and to take hold. Tanner takes *Portnoy* and Bellow's *Herzog* (both 'amazing monologues by recumbent figures') as examples of the process: 'Both novels, in their different ways, have something of this dual aspect of being at once desperate disencumberings and cherished re-evocations. Memory becomes an ambiguous phenomenon and both Bellow and Roth seem to get rid of something by getting hold of it.'[3] Portnoy asks: 'Is it the process, Doctor, or is it what we call "the material"? All I do is complain, the repugnance seems bottomless, and I'm beginning to wonder if maybe enough isn't enough' (*PC*, p. 105). We are what we eat, and all our lives we never finish getting hold of stuff to turn into ourselves, and then getting rid of it: so with the relation between experience, memory and selfhood. As the analyst has to 'get to the bottom' of this relation, so the novelist has to find a form for it.

The process of consumption and 'letting go' inside Roth's fiction is paralleled by his own processes as a writer. He is a self-conscious editor, corrector and critic of his own work. Writing about Roth is rendered at once easy and difficult by the fact that he has already said about himself much of what needs to be said. His collection of essays, *Reading Myself and Others* (1975), contains an interview 'conducted with myself'. In the last two novels he re-uses his novelist character Nathan Zuckerman, who in *The Ghost Writer* (1979) 'is' the young Jewish author of the *Goodbye, Columbus* stories, and in *Zuckerman Unbound* 'is' the suddenly successful and notorious author of *Portnoy*. It would be naïve to read Roth's novels as autobiographical – Tony Tanner borrows William Carlos Williams's phrase 'fictionalized recall' to describe them. But he *is* his own ghost writer, processing and reprocessing as 'useful fictions' the material he has consumed, and so, like Tarnopol the novelist in *My Life as a Man*, continually struggling 'to describe myself'. In this continuing employment of fiction as 'useful' self-description, there is a change from the early works (*Goodbye, Columbus*, *Letting Go*, *When She Was Good*), in which the characters' struggles are contained within a solid, externalized reality with fixed moral and social values, to the more 'Rothian' works of the late sixties and seventies (*Portnoy's Complaint*, *The Breast*, *My Life as a Man*, *The Professor of Desire*), in which the characters' self-describing, self-conscious voices *are* the narrative, and the writer ceases to be separable from his material. More recently, in *The Ghost Writer* and *Zuckerman Unbound*, the 'narcissistic' letting go of

17

the novelist/narrator/analysand is cunningly distanced by formal controls that place the subject's predicament in an ironic light. In spite of these interesting formal developments, however, Roth's personal fictions (and I am excluding here his political satires, *Our Gang* and *The Great American Novel*) are consistently concerned with the struggle of the self to describe and thereby to fulfil itself.

Roth's reprocessing of his own material is craftily illustrated by the reference in *The Ghost Writer* to Henry James's story 'The Middle Years', which is read by Lonoff and Zuckerman, the old novelist and the young one. James's dying novelist in the story is 'a passionate corrector', 'never able to arrive at a final form'. Lonoff is the same: he can write twenty-seven drafts of a single short story (' "To get it wrong," said Lonoff, "so many times." ') and cannot even read a magazine article without underlining and annotating it. And he occurs in a novel in which Roth is revising and re-using his own career as a writer as a fictional subject. Just as Portnoy nauseates himself by his own endless regurgitating – 'I'm beginning to wonder if maybe enough isn't enough' (*PC*, p. 105) – so Lonoff the novelist feels weariness and disgust at his compulsion endlessly to annotate, correct and reprocess his material. It is a form of self-abuse.

Self-disgust and self-consciousness are, then, essential ingredients in the subject-matter and the process of Roth's fiction. But the fiction and the fictional characters are also playful, energetic and full of stylish comic bravado. There is a multiple conflict between correction and creation, law and libido, restraint and letting go, nausea and appetite, in every aspect of Roth's work. This is perfectly summed up in his references to Kafka, whom Roth always writes about brilliantly. In *The Professor of Desire*, his professor, on a visit to Prague, finds that the erotic blockages, the proscriptions of the superego, which frustrate him (and other American Jewish intellectuals), are translated into real, external blockages. 'It's Kafka', the citizens of Prague tell each other after 1968: the blockages that Kafka describes in, for instance, *The Castle* ('a book engaged at every level with not reaching a climax', the professor says) have

18

become their daily life. The professor's own struggle between ethics and desire is imaged in the story he tells his girlfriend:

'Do you know what Kafka said to the man he shared an office with at the insurance company? At lunchtime he saw the fellow eating his sausage and Kafka is supposed to have shuddered and said, "The only fit food for a man is half a lemon!"' (*PD*, p. 141)

Roth has an essay on Kafka which takes its title from Kafka's story 'The Hunger Artist'.[4] 'I always wanted you to admire my fasting,' says the neglected 'fasting showman', who has prided himself on the length of his fasts – easy for him, since he dislikes eating – but who finds himself no longer remarkable in a time of universal hunger (the story is of Berlin in 1924). Then he dies, and the circus overseer replaces him, in the same cage, with a hungry, healthy young panther, 'the joy of life' streaming 'with such ardent passion from his throat that for the onlookers it was not easy to stand the shock of it' (*RMAO*, p. 229). Roth finds the story illustrative of Kafka's 'habit of obedience and renunciation; also, his own distaste for the diseased and reverence for strength, appetite, and health' (*RMAO*, p. 229).

The hunger artist and the hungry panther – half a lemon, or a sausage – are useful opposing images for what happens in Roth's books. He repeatedly describes his subject as being individuals struggling to get through and beyond the boundaries that seem to be set down for them. He links the subdued *When She Was Good* (1967) and the exhibitionist *Portnoy* by relating them both to the characters in the *Goodbye, Columbus* stories, 'each of whom is seen making a conscious, deliberate, even willful choice *beyond* the boundary lines of his life' (*RMAO*, p. 25). He compares *Portnoy* with *The Breast* (1972) by describing both as a struggle between 'the measured self' and 'the insatiable self', 'the accommodating self vs. the ravenous self' (*RMAO*, p. 64). In his central essay, the 'self-interview' which takes *The Great American Novel* (1973) as its starting point, he locates the core of all his work as 'the problematical nature of moral authority and of social restraint and regulation ... the question of who or what shall have influence and jurisdiction over one's life.' The essay goes on:

> The question of moral sovereignty, as it is examined in *Letting Go*, *Portnoy's Complaint*, and *The Breast*, is really a question of the kind of commandment the hero of each book will issue to himself; here the skepticism is directed inward, upon the hero's ambiguous sense of personal imperatives and taboos. I can even think of these characters – Gabe Wallach, Alexander Portnoy, and David Kepesh – as three stages of a single explosive projectile that is fired into the barrier that forms one boundary of the individual's identity and experience: that barrier of personal inhibition, ethical conviction and plain, old monumental fear beyond which lies the moral and psychological unknown. Gabe Wallach crashes up against the wall and collapses; Portnoy proceeds on through the fractured mortar, only to become lodged there, half in, half out. It remains for Kepesh to pass right on through the bloodied hole, and out the other end, into no-man's land. (*RMAO*, pp. 78–9)

The games-playing metaphor, 'crashing through the wall', recalls the most 'blocked', the most enraged and ravenous of all American heroes, Melville's Ahab, in a speech that is parodied in Roth's games-playing fiction *The Great American Novel*.

> 'Hark ye yet again – the little lower layer. All visible objects, man, are but as pasteboard masks. But in each event – in the living act, the undoubted deed – there, some unknown but still reasoning thing put forth the moulding of its features from behind the unreasoning mask. If man will strike, strike through the mask! How can the prisoner reach outside except by thrusting through the wall? To me, the white whale is that wall, shoved near to me. . . . Talk not to me of blasphemy, man; I'd strike the sun if it insulted me. . . . Who's over me? Truth has no confines.'[5]

Ahab's furious resolution to redefine himself beyond 'determined' limits is encompassed by Ishmael's contemplative, accommodating inquiry into the nature of existence, and versions of that dualism find their way repeatedly into American literature. Roth, like Melville, pursues the alternatives through the frequent use of doubles, *alter egos*, mentors, and opposing authorities who point the 'complaining' characters towards their refusals and choices. There is a clear parallel between what his characters choose and struggle with, and what sorts of novels he writes – and in what order.

Roth has frequently said that he wrote *Portnoy's Complaint* as a reaction against the 'moral seriousness' of his own and others' novels of the 1950s and early 1960s (*RMAO*, p. 193). His two closest friends, he says, are 'Sheer Playfulness and Deadly Seriousness' (*RMAO*, p. 101), and, though his early models may have been Flaubert and James, he owes quite as much allegiance to the likes of 'Henny Youngman, a Jewish nightclub and vaudeville comic' (*RMAO*, p. 74). One of his 'continuing problems', he said in 1973, has been

> to find the means to be true to these seemingly inimical realms of experience that I am strongly attached to by temperament and training – the aggressive, the crude, and the obscene, at one extreme, and something a good deal more subtle and, in every sense, refined at the other. (*RMAO*, p. 76)

The predicament, he goes on to say, is not his alone. He cites the essay of 1939 by Philip Rahv[6] which divided American writers into the 'paleface' and the 'redskin'. The 'paleface' – Henry James, T. S. Eliot – comes from the 'thin, solemn, semiclerical culture of Boston and Concord', 'hankers after religious norms' and 'moves in an exquisite moral atmosphere'. The 'redskin' – Walt Whitman, Mark Twain, Thomas Wolfe – comes from 'the lowlife world of the frontier and the big city'; his 'reactions are primarily emotional, spontaneous, and lacking in personal culture'; at his worst 'he is a vulgar anti-intellectual'. Roth describes a process in post-war America whereby 'a lot of redskins . . . went off to universities and infiltrated the departments of English' (*RMAO*, p. 76). There they produced what Roth wittily calls 'the redface', a writer who feels '*fundamentally ill-at-ease in, and at odds with*' both

21

the world of his background (very probably urban Jewish) and the world of respectable, Gentile academe. The result is, in his own work, 'a self-conscious and deliberate zig-zag', each book 'veering sharply away from the one before' (*RMAO*, p. 77).

Though the alternation between high seriousness and vaude-ville, between restraint and letting go, makes a clear pattern of development in Roth's work, I propose, in this short book, to approach his fiction thematically. As this introductory chapter has suggested, Roth's interest in consumption, in literary and psychological self-consciousness, in appetite and renunciation, in 'crashing through the wall', is consistent, and runs through very different kinds of narratives. He sets these ideas, over and over again, in the context of the middle-class urban Jewish-American family, and it is with this context that a more specific account of Philip Roth's work needs to begin.

2

'NATHAN DEDALUS':
JEWISH SONS, JEWISH NOVELISTS,
JEWISH JOKES

Philip Roth looks back on himself in youth as

> a good, responsible, well-behaved boy, controlled (rather willingly) by the social regulations of the self-conscious and orderly lower-middle-class neighborhood where I had been raised, and mildly constrained still by the taboos that had filtered down to me, in attenuated form, from the religious orthodoxy of my immigrant grandparents. (*RMAO*, pp. 3–4)

His paternal grandparents had emigrated from Austria-Hungary; his mother came of a native Jewish-American family. Roth was born (on 19 March 1933) in Newark, New Jersey, his father an insurance salesman; he attended Weequahic High School in Newark and then, for a year, Newark College, Rutgers University – Neil Klugman's university in *Goodbye, Columbus*. From 1951 to 1954 he went to Bucknell University to take his BA in English; in this Gentile Pennsylvanian institution he felt, he has said, 'like a Houyhnhnm who has strayed on to the campus from *Gulliver's Travels*'.[7] He took his MA at the University of Chicago (reflected in *Letting Go*). In 1955 he enlisted in the army and worked in the Public Information Office in Washington; his discharge with a back injury became the inspiration for the story 'Novotny's Pain'. From 1956 he was teaching and doing a PhD at Chicago, and his stories were beginning to appear. After the publication and success in 1959 of *Goodbye, Columbus*, he established a pattern of writing and teaching (at Iowa, Princeton and Pennsylvania) which was to continue even after the enormous notoriety and acclaim that greeted *Portnoy's Complaint* in 1969. Roth was married in 1959 and separated in 1962; his wife died in a car crash in 1968. After *Portnoy*, he moved out of New York to the New England countryside, and now divides his time between America and England.

Roth's Jewish-American childhood is the basis for his fiction; his journey outwards, through success as a writer (which itself necessitated the 'betrayal' of that childhood), from the Jewish-American home to an international acculturation, is always his subject. In describing himself as a 'redface', embarrassedly oscillating between high seriousness and vaudeville knockabout, feeling 'fundamentally ill-at-ease in, and at odds with' both his childhood and his adult environment, Roth is describing, in particular, the self-consciousness of the modern Jewish-American writer. From 'The Conversion of the Jews' (1958) right through to *Zuckerman Unbound* (1981), Roth's novels, stories and essays treat and make terms with Jewishness: not so much forging, after Joyce, 'the *un*created conscience of my race' but finding inspiration in 'a conscience that has been created and undone a hundred times in this century alone' (*RMAO*, p. 221). In the shadow of what Roth, with some weariness, calls 'this myriad of prototypes', his fiction has had to find its own way of describing how to be (in turn) a Jewish son, a Jewish adult and a Jewish writer. If 'the Judaization of American culture'[8] presents a difficulty for the writer, that intrinsic difficulty is exacerbated by the orthodox 'timidity and paranoia' (*RMAO*, p. 150) directed against any writer who is felt to be 'informing' on the Jews. And to be classified as yet another example of a thriving genre – whether as a 'black humorist' out of Nathanael West, in company with Bruce Jay Friedman or Joseph Heller, or as a comic monologuist in the style of Lenny Bruce or Woody Allen,[9] or as a 'campus novelist' ('The English Instructor As Hero: Two Novels by Roth and Malamud'[10]), or as one of an indistinguishable trio of Jewish moralists ('Bellowmalamudroth and the American Jewish Genre – Alive and Well'[11]) – can be just as daunting as to be attacked for 'seeking only to cheapen the people he writes about'.[12]

Of course, Roth is part of the cultural change – colourfully described by Leslie Fiedler in his critical study *Waiting for the End* (1964) – which produced the post-war 'triumph' of the Jewish novelist in America. He began to be published at the end of the 1950s, the decade when Jewish-American fiction had become important for its treatment of the history of persecution and of the process of assimilation, and when the Jewish-American hero – victim, survivor, joker and voice of moral conscience – had come of age. Comparisons with Saul Bellow and Bernard Malamud, or, going further back, with Nathanael West and Henry Roth, can usefully be made, especially with Philip Roth's earlier works; and Roth has made many of them himself. But he began later than the writers he was often grouped with, and has from the start been an uncomfortable, and discomforting, part of the tradition. He has always wanted 'to alter a system of responses to "Jewish fiction"' (*RMAO*, p. 157) and not to be thought of, either by literary critics or by rabbis, as a writer who must be judged only in terms of his Jewishness. It is a trap he has repeatedly fictionalized. The Jewish writer must treat his own background and use what he knows best; but he wants, as well, to 'fly by those nets' and be 'unbound'. It is a form of Portnoy's complaint:

> I am not in this boat alone, oh no, I am on the biggest troop ship afloat . . . only look in through the portholes and see us there, stacked to the bulkheads in our bunks, moaning and groaning with such pity for ourselves, the sad and watery-eyed sons of Jewish parents, sick to the gills from rolling through these heavy seas of guilt – so I sometimes envision us, me and my fellow wailers, melancholics, and wise guys, still in steerage, like our forebears. . . . Will this fucking ship ever stop pitching? When? *When*, so that we can leave off complaining how sick we are – and go out into the air, and live! (*PC*, pp. 132–3)

The metaphor of the second-generation immigrant ship full of complaining Jewish sons wanting to get off is a joke that applies as much to writers as to sons. Roth's self-conscious literary dualism – good taste versus vulgarity, restraint versus licence – is analogous to the 'Abel and Cain' predicament of all his Jewish sons. Literary highmindedness was the product of the 'penchant for ethical striving that I had absorbed as a Jewish child' (*RMAO*, p. 71). Literary anarchy, vulgarity and obscenity were quite as much the product of Yiddish wisecracks, 'lascivious neighborhood gossip', 'unconstrained Jewish living-room clowns' (*RMAO*, p. 75), a rhetoric and a folklore that made up the 'demythologizing' side of the Jewish-American childhood. Rival figures of authority – the proud father, the caring mother, the preventing rabbi, the irreverent luckless *shlemiel*, the busybodying *kibitzer*, the black-sheep uncle – provided alternative possibilities for 'selfhood'. What kind of son shall the Jewish son choose to be? The '"Jewboy" (with all that word signifies to Jew and Gentile alike about aggression, appetite, and marginality)' or 'the "nice Jewish boy" (and what that epithet implies about repression, respectability, and social acceptance)' (*RMAO*, p. 31)? Portnoy's socially responsible job, at the age of 33, as Assistant Commissioner for Mayor Lindsay's New York Commission on Human Opportunity, so drastically at odds both with his parents' treatment of him as a 15-year-old boy and with his reckless pursuit of *shiksa* pussy, is the perfect example of the Jewish son attempting to sublimate his 'bad' desires with a 'good' professional life. (Though Portnoy's job of solving the television quiz scandals and of mediating between 'poor minorities and established WASP society'[13] is as demeaning a service to the Gentile American world as his father's selling of insurance to black families in Newark.) Portnoy's fears are always of being found out: of headlines 'revealing my filthy secrets to a shocked and disapproving world' (*PC*, p. 197) – 'JEW SMOTHERS DEB WITH COCK' – of the family rabbi revealing his secrets to an assembled audience in hell, of the bathroom door swinging open to reveal 'the saviour of mankind, drool running down his chin, absolutely gaa-gaa in the eyes, and his prick firing salvos at the light bulb. A bad boy!' (*PC*, p. 226).

In 'How Did You Come to Write That Book, Anyway?' Roth

gives an interesting account (*RMAO*, pp. 29–37) of how *Portnoy's Complaint* evolved through a literary negotiation between alternative kinds of Jewishness. The first project was a 'dreamy, humorous' draft of a novel called *The Jewboy*, which treated growing up in Newark as a species of folklore. Then came an attempt at a realist play called *The Nice Jewish Boy*. Then (after the completion of the serious novel *When She Was Good*) Roth wrote a long, blasphemous, scatological, 'tasteless' monologue containing a section on adolescent masturbation, and, at much the same time, 'a strongly autobiographical piece of fiction' about his own childhood, provisionally and predictably entitled *Portrait of the Artist*. This incorporated a family of upstairs neighbours called the Portnoys, who closely resembled a typical Jewish family described in an earlier essay on Jewish stereotypes. In that family (which Roth repeatedly encountered in stories written by Jewish graduates in the University of Iowa's Writing Workshop) the Jewish son is 'watched' by his mother, 'asphyxiated' by domestic warmth, and longs to be initiated by his Gentile schoolfriend into the sexual temptations offered by the *shiksas* – those girls whom Portnoy generically refers to as Thereal McCoy. With the 'releasing' of the Portnoys from their 'supporting roles', and the discovery of Portnoy's voice '(more accurately, his mouth)', *Portnoy's Complaint* at last took shape. But it had taken six or more years of experimenting with the rival claims of fantasy and realism, folklore[14] and autobiography, seriousness and scatology, for the analysand's monologue 'perhaps to begin'.

The writer's difficulties are the son's: Roth's choices of style and manner are equivalent to the son's choice between being the 'nice', 'good' Jewish boy, normal, achieving, accommodating, successful; or else the 'Jewfreak',[15] refusing, complaining, neurotic, seasick, outraged and outrageous. All Jewish fiction, Roth tells us, oscillates between appetite and renunciation, between 'I want' and 'I am horrified'. 'In Portnoy the disapproving moralist who says "I am horrified" will not disappear when the libidinous slob shows up screaming "I want!"' (*RMAO*, p. 219).

*

Portnoy's Complaint makes the most intense and extravagant statement of the choice in Roth's fiction, for writer and character alike, between two kinds of Jewishness. But all the work leading up to *Portnoy* has dealt with versions of that novel's dilemma. Roth's early stories of the 1950s are, in energetically various ways, stories of resistance or accommodation, of Jewish characters saying, or not being able to say, 'No, I refuse' (*RMAO*, p. 149). The models are not necessarily Jewish – Stephen Dedalus's 'Non serviam' and Bartleby the Scrivener's 'I prefer not to' both have a bearing – but the idea is placed very firmly in the Jewish-American context. Even the early uncollected stories show promise of this: in 'The Contest for Aaron Gold' (1955) Roth quickly establishes the rough philistinism of the summer camp where Aaron is a misfit, better at pottery than at basketball;[16] in the surreal sketch 'The Day It Snowed' (1954) the anxiety of the boy whose family is disappearing bit by bit is set in an adult world of mysterious rules and secrets:

> There was just the crying again like when Aunt Wilma disappeared, and there was his mother whispering to his step-father as if she had a secret, and from the look on her face when she whispered, Sydney could tell the secret was about Uncle Carl. Whenever she saw Sydney watching her she would stop telling the secret, but once Sydney did hear her say to his step-father 'Don't be a fool – at least let us spare the child,' and so nobody had to tell Sydney that Uncle Carl had disappeared too.[17]

Both stories end with the boy running away from his teacher or family.

In *Goodbye, Columbus* (1959), his first collection, containing the title novella and five short stories, the revolts are more circumscribed, the net of family and community more closely drawn around the central figure. The distinction of these stories is their attentive, comical display of social detail – army talk in 'Defender of the Faith', suburban Jewish life in 'Goodbye, Columbus' and 'Eli, the Fanatic', schoolboy behaviour in 'The Conversion of the Jews' and 'You Can't Tell a Man by the Song he Sings'. In 'Goodbye, Columbus' Neil Klugman describes the park outside the Newark public library with a charmed devotion to local minutiae which springs, as he says, from 'a deep knowledge of Newark, an attachment so rooted that it could not help but branch out into affection' (*GC*, p. 22). That, of course, is his and the author's predicament: like Stephen Dedalus, he is emotionally and aesthetically bound to the environment he wants, urgently, to resist. In fact Neil Klugman, as indecisive as Prufrock ('I haven't planned a thing in five years'), does not go far in his revolt – just from his surrogate mother's kitchen and the Newark library to the household of the Patimkins, wealthy suburbanized Jews ('Since when do Jewish people live in Short Hills? They couldn't be real Jews believe me,' says his Aunt Gladys (*GC*, p. 41)), and then back again. Even so, the short journey from his ethnic roots in the 'Jewish ghetto' to the world of secularized, Americanized Patimkin wealth is enough to disturb Neil's sense of identity. The newly rich Patimkins have moved up from Newark into gentility on the back of the wartime kitchen-sink boom and now represent the 1950s American dream of affluence. They are 'real' enough in terms of goods and clothes and games: 'Oh Patimkin! Fruit grew in their refrigerator and sporting goods dropped from their trees' (*GC*, p. 31). The family is caught in unforgiving detail, from little Julie's cheating ('Mr Patimkin had taught his daughters that free throws were theirs for the asking' (*GC*, p. 20)), to the neurotic mother's synagogue snobbery, and the son Ron's mindlessly assimilated dedication to the all-American campus (the appropriately chosen university at Columbus, Ohio) and to all-American gamesmanship.

Neil's gravitation towards the 'prize' of material goods, and his half-baked attempts to liberate the attractive Patimkin daughter Brenda from her family by making her get a diaphragm, are compared (rather mawkishly) to the escapist dreams of the small black boy who comes into the library every day to look at a book of Gauguin's paintings ('Ain't that the fuckin *life*?'). But 'Goodbye, Columbus' doesn't get beyond being a satire on the alternative family lives that are observed by the Jewish boy discovering America. That Neil is missing a sense of self ('I sat down in my Brooks Brothers shirt and pronounced my own name out loud' (*GC*, p. 47)) is just touched on at the end when, the affair over, he gazes into the window of Harvard's Lamont Library ('Patimkin sinks in the rest rooms') and lets his gaze 'push through' his own image in the glass to 'a broken wall of books, imperfectly shelved' (*GC*, p. 97). Then, in time for the Jewish New Year, he catches the train back to Newark and his job. A faint suggestion has been made, which will be taken up in later books, that an alternative to the disappointing 'American dream' of material wealth and sexual liberation may be found in the 'useful fictions' of books and art.

In some of the other stories in *Goodbye, Columbus*, the attempt to 'push through' into a real choice of 'selfhood' is more powerfully made. Though these are comic dilemmas, with an eye for absurd disruptions of normal life – the boy up on the roof of the *shul* making everyone kneel down like Gentiles, the guilty married man caught with his trousers down by the entire family – in each case a serious, self-made crisis faces the central character. Little Ozzie Freedman, in 'The Conversion of the Jews', chooses to resist orthodoxy by refusing to accept Rabbi Binder's statement that the virgin birth is an impossibility ('You don't know anything about God!' (*GC*, p. 105)). Sergeant Marx in 'Defender of the Faith' refuses to be compromised by Private Grossbart's self-interested appeals for Jewish solidarity in a Gentile world ('Let the goyim clean the floors!' (*GC*, p. 123)). Moved at first by natural sympathies arising from his 'deep memory' of a Bronx childhood, Marx negotiates awkwardly between the Jews and the army officers, in some comical interchanges ('"Jewish parents, sir – they're apt to be more protective than you expect" . . . "Marx, here, tells me Jews have a tendency to be pushy"' (*GC*, p. 126)). But Grossbart and his cronies make a fool of him, and he realizes that he must free himself from what is, in effect, racial persecution 'by another Jew' (*RMAO*, p. 157). Epstein, in a less interesting story, tries, farcically, to spring the family trap – dead son, fat nagging wife, grimly 'politicized' daughter – by having an affair with the widow next door. An embarrassing infection and a badly timed heart attack put paid to this bid for freedom: 'Lou, you'll live normal, won't you?' his wife cries in the ambulance (*GC*, p. 165).

In 'Eli, the Fanatic' the lawyer (like Sergeant Marx, a negotiator) is 'burdened by the message' he has to take from the secularized Jews of suburban Woodenton to Mr Tzuref (the name means 'troubles') who has opened a *yeshivah* (Orthodox elementary school) in this 'assimilated', 'progressive' community. Both Eli the lawyer and Sergeant Marx are challenged by potential 'doubles', who may be persecutors or saviours. In Roth these 'doubles', who will recur, are always Jewish – like Susskind, the Jew in Bernard Malmamud's story 'Last Mohican', who makes Fidelman responsible for him 'because you are a man. Because you are a Jew', and unlike the more usual situation in Saul Bellow's *The Victim*, where Asa Leventhal is persecuted by the Gentile Allbee. Pulling at Eli on one side are his secularized neighbours ('This Abraham in the Bible was going to kill his own *kid* for a sacrifice. . . . Today a guy like that they'd lock him up!' (*GC*, p. 200)) and his pregnant wife, who reads Freud and wants things to be 'normal'. Pushing at him from the other side is the insistent presence of Mr Tzuref ('Aach! You are us, we are you!' (*GC*, p. 192)) and his unassimilated, black-robed 'greenhorn' assistant. The satire on wealthy suburban Jewish life is more complex here than in 'Goodbye, Columbus'. Eli knows that this community is peaceful and safe, 'a place for families, even Jewish families'. 'It was what his parents had asked for in the Bronx, and his grandparents in Poland, and theirs in Russia or Austria, or wherever else they'd fled to or from' (*GC*, p. 202). He half shares its rejection of the *yeshivah* and the greenie, reminders of the victimized, suffering Jewish past. But that orthodoxy (which others of Roth's characters, like Ozzie Freedman, resist) goes deeper than anything in the safe suburban landscape of the 'Stop 'n Shop', the 'Bit-in-Teeth Restaurant' and 'Roger's Beauty Shoppe'. Eli begins to identify with the poor greenie, exchanges clothes with him and, bearing 'the terrible weight of the stranger's strange hat' (*GC*, p. 206), is carted off, after visiting his newborn son, to the community's asylum, feeling a 'deep blackness' in his soul.

31

The story, like Flannery O'Connor's 'Revelation' or 'The Enduring Chill',[18] works towards a moment of visionary acceptance; it also invokes Hawthorne's tales of the true man's social ostracism (such as 'The Minister's Black Veil'). Ozzie races to the edge of the roof, asking himself 'Is it me? Is it me ME ME ME ME! It has to be me – but is it?' (*GC*, p. 106), and longs, like a juvenile Jewish Ahab, to 'rip open the sky, plunge his hands through' (*GC*, p. 112). Sergeant Marx 'accepts' his fate when he rejects Grossbart. Similarly, Eli remakes his self against the will of the community, and in so doing lets go of 'normality'. These are not dignified or triumphant choices: Ozzie has to plummet down from his moment of hubris into the 'net' glowing below 'like an overgrown halo', and Eli's struggle to decide what kind of Jew he is ends in madness.

These stories aroused enormous controversy among conservative and orthodox Jewish circles, especially when *Goodbye, Columbus* won the National Book Award in 1960. The attacks on Roth by rabbis ('a distorted image of the basic values of Orthodox Judaism'; *RMAO*, p. 135), angry correspondents ('will do irreparable damage to the Jewish people'; RMAO, p. 145) and Jewish literary critics ('Roth's characters are coarse, crafty, ugly, crude, common, brutish and low-minded precisely because *they are Jews*'[19]) were at once put to use as literary material. 'Because recognition – and, with it, opposition – came to me almost immediately, I seem . . . to have felt called upon both to assert a literary position and to defend my moral flank the instant after I had managed to take my first steps,' he noted (*RMAO*, p. viii). *Portnoy's Complaint* is a form of assertion and defence. The Israeli girl who kicks and derides Portnoy and takes exception to his beastliness, his 'self-hate' and his obscenities is one of Roth's literary critics. Before that, he had defended himself rather solemnly, in the 1963 essay 'Writing About Jews', where he argues that the time for living in fear of Gentile persecution is over:

The cry 'Watch out for the goyim!' at times seems more the expression of an unconscious wish than of a warning: Oh that they were out there, so that we could be together in here!

32

A rumour of persecution, a taste of exile, might even bring with it that old world of feelings and habits – something to replace the new world of social accessibility and moral indifference, the world which tempts all our promiscuous instincts, and where one cannot always figure out what a Jew is that a Christian is not. (*RMAO*, pp. 149–50)

His own fiction, he claims, does for the Jewish image what Ralph Ellison's *Invisible Man* does for the blacks. It is 'an expression of moral consciousness' (*RMAO*, p. 137).

To have been attacked by the Jewish establishment was nothing unusual for a Jewish writer if he was not Leon Uris or Harry Golden. Leslie Fiedler, reviewing *Goodbye, Columbus*, called 'the accusation of anti-Semitism' 'the young Jewish writer's initial accolade'[20] and was later to describe the 'anti-conformism' of the contemporary Jewish writer as having become, in its turn, a brand of conformity.[21] Roth recognizes that 'the opposition was instructive',[22] and by now it has become essential to his treatment of the Jewish son and writer. The last two novels, *The Ghost Writer* and *Zuckerman Unbound* (set in 1956 and 1969), are both, retrospectively, about the son's need to revolt from the community in order to master it as material. Both turn on a comic confrontation between the writer's need for secrecy, aloofness and self-determination and the threatening, importunate criticisms of family, fans, reviewers and nuts on the sidewalk. Both give comic (but probably not much exaggerated) versions of those angry letters of the sixties: 'Can you honestly say that there is anything in your short story that would not warm the heart of a Julius Streicher or a Joseph Goebbels?' (*GW*, p. 91); 'Dear Mr Zuckerman: It is hardly possible to write of Jews with more bile and contempt and hatred' (*ZU*, p. 59). In *The Ghost Writer* the parallel predicaments of son and writer merge: it is Nathan's father, furious and heartbroken at Nathan's first story (which draws on the same sort of neighbourhood folklore as did Roth's 'Epstein'), who speaks, though tenderly, in the voice of Roth's early critics: 'It's not your fault that you don't know what Gentiles think when they read something like this. . . . I wonder if you fully understand just how very little love there is in this world for Jewish people' (*GW*, p. 82).

Nathan's sad father closes the circle that begins with Rabbi Binder. Those figures of authority – Jewish fathers, teachers, critics – whom Roth had, in life, to resist from the earliest stages of his profession, have since then played a consistent part in his fictions. In all his works so far, Roth's Jewish families, like the Dedalus family in Joyce's *Portrait of the Artist as a Young Man*, are the material for, and the obstacles to, the fully adult writer who can master and describe himself and his world. In order to be a writer one must cease to be a son. The Jewish son who grows up to be the novelist is 'in possession' of his material, but he is also 'unbound', dispossessed, 'no longer any man's son' (*ZU*, p. 224).

*

Between *Goodbye, Columbus* and *Portnoy's Complaint*, the Jewish son's struggle for freedom and self-possession takes the form of a long, 'realist' narrative, *Letting Go* (1962), in which his predicament is split between two central characters. *Letting Go* begins with a dying mother's letter to her son ('I was always doing things for another's good. The rest of my life I could push and pull people with a clear conscience' (*LG*, p. 2)) and then divides itself between two Jewish sons' attempts to get free of all that pushing and pulling. Both Gabe Wallach and Paul Herz are teachers of literature, both are involved with Gentile girls, but Gabe, well-off, confused, unable to commit himself, trails a wreckage of relationships foundered on bad faith, while Paul struggles grimly to be a real *mensch*, 'a man of duty', and to make his marriage to the neurotic Libby (a Jewish convert) work and last. This, Roth's first long novel, has not found a structure to suit it. Like its stultified characters, the narrative gets bogged down in long, detailed set-pieces – Martha Reganhart's messy Gentile household, campus 'characters', the Herz family in Brooklyn – strong in themselves, but clogging up the essential idea of Gabe and Paul as *alter egos*. By the time Gabe begins to act decisively (in getting a child for Paul and Libby to adopt), the shape of the novel has been submerged.

But Gabe's resistance to the 'overwhelming love' showered on him by his widowed dentist father, a weeper and wisecracker whose 'passions ached him' and who spent his married life, like Mr Portnoy, 'constipating himself', is strongly felt as an alternative to Paul's painful choice between being a good husband and being a good son to his anxious father, a failed small businessman sitting in his BarcaLounger in Brooklyn expecting a heart attack. Both families are surrounded with a mass of half-ironic, half-tender details, lavished on Mr Wallach's Thanksgiving party, or the Herzes' neighbours, or Paul's uncle Asher — in all of which the two young humanities teachers struggle on their hooks. Paul's cynical, shabbily hedonistic uncle tells him:

> 'Listen to Uncle Shmuck, will you? Things come and go, and you have got to be a receptacle, let them pass right through. Otherwise death will be a misery for you, boy; I'd hate to see it. . . . Wait and accept and learn to pull the hand away. *Don't clutch!* What is marriage, what is it but a pissy form of greed, a terrible, disgusting ambitiousness.' (*LG*, p. 83)

Whether the Jewish son is trying to escape the clutch of family and marriage, or is conscious that he is himself desperately clutching — whether he is trying to be let go or to let go — he must suffer. The punishment may be sprung on the complaining victim in bizarre, surreal form, like Novotny's undiagnosable back pain, which comes upon him after he has been drafted into the army and is waiting to go to Korea ('What had he done in life to deserve this? What had he done, from the day he had grown out of short pants, but everything that was asked of him?' (*PRR*, p. 270)), or David Kepesh's transformation into a breast ('HOW COULD IT HAVE HAPPENED? IN THE ENTIRE HISTORY OF THE HUMAN RACE, WHY PROFESSOR KEPESH?' (*PRR*, p. 456)). Its causes may be pursued through a profusion of realistic detail, or turned into exhaustive, agonized jokes. But the versions and descriptions have to be unremittingly regurgitated.

In *My Life as a Man* (1974), the sufferings of the Jewish son, husband and novelist are compulsively reworked in a series of

'Useful Fictions', alternative versions of the novelist Peter Tarnopol's 'true story', in which he attempts to describe himself and to exorcize his obsession with his destructive marriage. In the fragmentary narratives of *My Life as a Man* the novelist is at once victim and analyst, confessor and interpreter of his own sufferings. Tarnopol's struggle to describe himself begins with the comic narrative 'Salad Days', in which Nathan Zuckerman is the protected, petted son of a 'bewildering dynamo of a protector' (like Mr Herz, a repeatedly failing small businessman) and an over-encouraging mother, with a brother whose teenage boasting collapses into domesticity with 'flatchested Sheila, the dental technician'. The family dream of financial security comes true in 1949 'just as the family was falling apart'. Nathan's humanities course at college teaches him a new set of terms ('"irony" and "values" and "fate", "will and vision" and "authenticity", and, of course, "human"') which make him scornful of his parents and of Sharon Shatsky, the sexy daughter of Al 'the Zipper King' Shatsky, whose mind he despises but whom he debauches in earshot of their mothers: '"I want to be your whore," she whispered to him (without prompting too), while on the back terrace her mother told his mother how adorable Sharon looked in the winter coat they'd bought for her that afternoon' (*MLAM*, p. 27). In 'Courting Disaster', the second 'fiction', the father is a book-keeper and Nathan's childhood is taken up with arithmetical problems and luxurious illnesses, but the ingredients of the complaint are the same: the over-protective, anxious-making Jewish childhood leads to a painful split between conscience and libido. Nathan, whose professional life as a teacher is orderly but whose migraines 'signify' repression, 'courts disaster' by seeking out Lydia, a goy who has had the most cruel, untender childhood imaginable. He likes her because she has suffered. The marriage (like the marriages of his sister, who twice marries 'no-good' goys) ends with his running off to Italy with his stepdaughter and with Lydia's suicide, and is as disastrous (in soap-opera style) as anyone in search of punishment could desire.

The 'true story' of Tarnopol works as a critique on these

versions. His real brother and sister are highly successful, one as a rich West Coast society hostess, the other as a bighearted New York radical. In his fictions Tarnopol had wished on them versions of the mess he creates for himself by trying to match 'I want' with 'I am horrified'. Tarnopol wants to be 'good', to be 'humanish: manly, a man', like Bellow's hero trying to be 'a marvellous Herzog, a Herzog who, perhaps clumsily, tried to live out marvellous qualities vaguely comprehended.'[23] In fact, he is childish, hysterical, narcissistic, at the mercy of desire, fear and loathing. His marriage to Maureen, who defiles all the childhood taboos and destroys the order of his life, plunges him into an '*un*manning frenzy'. Later heroes may be less frantic than Portnoy or Tarnopol, but they are still guilty about their parents, still divided between wanting to be good, even 'marvellous', and plunging into the messy world of unprotected sensations. In *The Professor of Desire* (1977), the split is imaged by Kepesh's relationship with the libidinous Baumgarten: 'I am Baumgarten . . . caged in the kennels . . . while he is a Kepesh, oh, what a Kepesh! with his mouth frothing and his tongue lolling, leash slipped and running wild' (*PD*, p. 112). In *The Ghost Writer* (1979), the aspiring Jewish writer, looking for a literary father to replace the Newark foot doctor, chooses between the 'good', highminded, conscientious, reclusive Lonoff and the 'bad', sensual, jet-setting, self-publicizing Abranavel. In *Zuckerman Unbound* (1981), the successful unhappy Nathan, now the notorious author of *Carnovsky*, is called 'bastard' by his dying father. It is only in *The Breast* (1972, revised 1980) that the Jewish parents help their son towards fully adult selfhood. Kepesh, trying to come to terms with himself as a large mammary gland, realizes that his father's nobility and his late mother's determination have helped his acceptance of his fate. But this Jewish hero is allowed to exist only in an absurd, surrealist context: he is the hero of a joke.

*

As Freud tells us, the Jewish joke is a form of self-abuse. The old marriage-broker stories which Freud uses as examples of 'tendentious' jokes (outlets for aggression, hostility) direct what he calls 'rebellious criticism' against 'the subject himself' or 'someone in whom the subject has a share . . . the subject's own nation, for instance'.[24] The essential sadness of the Jewish joke – what Freud describes as the allusions they make to 'the manifold and hopeless miseries of the Jews' – has not been short of commentators. 'The Jew functions in his deepest imagination . . . as his own other, his own inferior, and he must consequently laugh at himself. . . . This is the famous Jewish humour.'[25] In Jewish stories 'laughter and trembling are so curiously intermingled that it is not easy to determine the relations of the two.'[26] 'I am the son in the Jewish joke – only it ain't no joke!' says Portnoy (*PC*, p. 39). *Portnoy*, like almost all of Roth's work, depends on the symbiosis of comedy and pain, on making play with suffering by means of 'parody, burlesque, slapstick, ridicule, insult, invective, lampoon, wisecrack' (*RMAO*, p. 30). Portnoy is doubly a self-abusing humorist: that is, he makes use to the full of the tradition of 'self-abuse' in the Jewish joke, and at the same time abuses the tradition. *Portnoy's Complaint* is more than the ultimate Jewish joke; it is a joke *against* Jewish humour. Roth's protest against the rabbi's or Jewish mother's self-limiting idea of Jewishness is the same as Portnoy's complaint at being trapped inside a Jewish joke.

Roth has said that the moment *Portnoy* became possible was the moment when he thought of casting the Marx Brothers in a film of *The Castle*, by 'that sit-down comic' Kafka: 'guilt, you see, as a comic idea' (*RMAO*, pp. 19–20). To call Kafka a 'sit-down comic' is not just to joke. Like Sholom Aleichem's or Isaac Bashevis Singer's folk-narrators, like Saul Bellow using the noisy, vigorous, aggressive voice of Augie March ('I started to laugh loudly. . . . Look at me, going everywhere!'[27]) or Stanley Elkin and his busy, boastful narrator in 'Alex and the Gipsy' ('I'm Alexander Main the Bailbondsman. . . . My conditions classic and my terms terminal'[28]), Roth is turning an oral tradition into a written one. The Marx Brothers, Lenny Bruce and Woody Allen are direct inheritors of Jewish story-telling and wisecracking; what Roth (and other Jewish writers) have to do is to turn that legacy into literature. Stanley Elkin's bereaved hero Greenspahn, in the story 'Criers and Kibitzers, Kibitzers and Criers' (1961), thinks of the *kibitzers* (meddlers, jokers) as men 'deaf to grief, winking confidentially at the others, their voices high-pitched in kidding or lowered in conspiracy to tell of triumphs, of men they knew downtown, of tickets fixed, or languishing goods moved suddenly and unexpectedly, of the windfall that was life', and of the criers as 'dependably lamenting their lives'.[29] Roth incorporates both kinds of voices, the clowns and the complainers, into his narratives, with apparent ease; but the process involves, as much as at any level of his work, that characteristic conflict between restraint and licence. Vulgar speech – 'the aggressive, the crude, and the obscene' (*RMAO*, p. 76) – has to be embedded in and disciplined by literary form.

Nathan Zuckerman's frantic fan (or would-be assassin) Alvin Pepler, ex-TV-quiz contestant and memorizer extraordinary of all the pop-song titles since 1940, is bowled over, in *Zuckerman Unbound*, by Nathan's repartees: 'Well, it's like the critics say, nobody can top you with the one-liner' (*ZU*, p. 27). Alvin, a victim of the American media, and another of the 'secret sharers' (a term for *alter egos* borrowed from Conrad) who dog Roth's Jewish 'heroes', is obsessed with Zuckerman as a media success, and draws attention to the least literary of Zuckerman's (and Roth's) qualities: the gag, the one-liner, the punchline. Many of Roth's best jokes, as Alvin tells Nathan, are one-liners: *Portnoy* is full of them, of course ('With a life like mine, Doctor, who needs dreams?' (*PC*, p. 186); 'She puts the id back in Yid, I put the *oy* back in *goy*' (*PC*, p. 236)). But, less obviously, so is the earnest realism of *Letting Go* ('You look nice, Paul. You got a nice expression on your face. Second violinist for the Krakow Philharmonic' (*LG*, p. 425)) and the elegant narrative of *The Ghost Writer* ('He was like California itself – to get there you had to take a plane' (*GW*, p. 53)). However deep the commitment to moral seriousness, great literature and good taste, pain and wisdom have continually to be registered through the cheap, 'vulgar' wisecrack – for all that Portnoy may expostulate: '*Oedipus Rex* is a famous tragedy, schmuck, not another joke!' (*PC*, p. 301).

39

The punchline that famously ends *Portnoy's Complaint* ('So,' [*said the doctor*]. 'Now vee may perhaps to begin. Yes?'), the one-liners for which Nathan Zuckerman is praised, are not, obviously, Roth's only comic ploys. In one long, brilliant story, 'On the Air', to which I shall return, Roth treats American reality as if it were a surreal radio show. But all of Roth's work, especially the first-person narratives, is full of jokes that refer to radio, film, stage and music hall. The function of the one-liners is to turn the characters into performers in a comedy routine, and, quite apart from the invitation to 'the Alexander Portnoy show', this is very often explicitly done. Tarnopol compares that unseemly trio, his id, ego and superego, to the Marx Brothers, his marriage to the squabbles of 'Blondie and Dagwood, or Maggie and Jiggs' (*MLAM*, p. 276), his 'father-and-son routine' to an Abbott and Costello dialogue, and he calls himself 'the Dagwood Bumstead of fear and trembling' (*MLAM*, p. 214). The most consistent complaint of Roth's heroes is at the comic parts they are forced to play. Tarnopol doesn't want to be in his soap opera. David Kepesh (who at one point describes himself as 'Raskolnikov as played by Pudd'nhead Wilson' (*PD*, p. 31)) dreads leaving the world of Chekhov for the world of Gogol (as he does in *The Breast*) and becoming 'the butt of a ridiculous, vicious, inexplicable joke!' (*PD*, p. 204). Nathan Zuckerman feels let down by Aristotle: 'He didn't mention anything about the theatre of the ridiculous in which I am now a leading character' (*ZU*, p. 95). And Portnoy – 'the Raskolnikov of jerking off' (*PC*, p. 21) – complains vociferously about the standard Jewish joke in which he finds himself trapped:

It *hoits*, you know, there is pain involved, a little human suffering is being felt. . . . The macabre is very funny on the stage – but not to live it, thank you! . . . I mean here's a joke for you, for instance. Three Jews are walking down the street, my mother, my father, and me. . . . Oh, why go on? Why be so obsessed like this? . . . laugh it all off, right? (*PC*, pp. 125–7)

David Kepesh as a breast, or Tarnopol in the throes of his

appalling marriage, realize themselves as protagonists in a long-running farce out of Gogol or Kafka, and *Portnoy* is full of 'situations', the imaginary (coming home blind with a guide dog after jerking off into his own eye, his mother screaming 'Jack, there's a dog in the house and I just washed the kitchen floor!' (*PC*, p. 204)) hardly less grotesque than the actual. Some of these anecdotes are told not of Portnoy but of other Jewish sons, whose fates confirm Portnoy's case. Athletic cousin Hershie's family thwarts his engagement to a blonde Gentile cheer-leader by telling her that Hershie has an incurable blood disease, and is consoled for his death in the war by being told 'At least he didn't leave you with a shikse wife' (*PC*, p. 66). Ronald Nimkin, 15 years old and all set to be a concert pianist, hangs himself in the bathroom with a note pinned to his 'nice stiffly laundered sports shirt': '*Mrs Blumenthal called. Please bring your mahjongg rules to the game tonight. Ronald*' (*PC*, p. 135).

The relish for illustrations, peripheral anecdotes, comic sidekicks, routines by minor characters, is there from the start. The funniest part of 'Goodbye, Columbus' is a long speech by a Jewish light-bulb salesman, Uncle Leo, the Willie Loman of the Patimkin family, bursting with good one-liners, on cabs ('All the time I'm riding I'm watching the meter. Even the pleasures I can't enjoy'), or on his few sexual excitements ('Aachhh! Everything good in my life I can count on my fingers' (*GC*, p. 83)). *Letting Go* comes alive with Uncle Asher's seedy bravado and with the malevolent, pathetic rows between two dingy old men, Korngold and Levy, an underwear salesman and a small-time crooked lawyer, tenants in the grim Detroit house where Paul and Libby live. Their comical, sad and loquacious accosting of Paul anticipates Alvin Pepler's buttonholing of Nathan. David Kepesh's serious pursuit of 'the true self at its truest' (*PD*, p. 199) is periodically enlivened and subverted by Baumgarten's erotic stories and by the unforgettable childhood example of Herbie Bratasky, the coarse Yiddish entertainer and exhibitionist who, among his other routines, could 'do' 'taking a leak, taking a crap, diarrhea – *and* unrolling the paper itself' (*PD*, p. 11). That the Portnoy family should have begun

41

life as upstairs neighbours in an autobiographical draft, comic sidekicks in a serious narrative, is appropriate. When Roth is at his most freewheeling, in the satires on America like 'On the Air', *Our Gang* and *The Great American Novel*, these comic routines take over the centre of the stage.

What obviously characterizes these comic turns is their unashamed use and re-use of Jewish stereotypes, and their brilliant display of spoken rhetoric. Roth's linguistic bravado is the most apparent side of his Jewishness, and, of all the contemporary Jewish-American writers, his incorporation of the Yiddish-American voice into fiction has been the most spectacular. Since the turn of the century, Jewish writers have been taking over the American language (outstanding examples of the process before Roth are Abraham Cahan's *The Rise of David Levinsky* (1917), Henry Roth's *Call It Sleep* (1935) and Daniel Fuchs's *Homage to Blenholt* (1936), all novels that draw heavily on spoken idioms) and creating a characteristic Jewish-American style. Irving Howe has described its ingredients as

> a yoking of opposites . . . street-energy with high-culture rhetoric; a strong infusion of Yiddish, not so much through the occasional use of a phrase or word as through ironic twistings . . . ; a rapid, nervous, breathless tempo, like the hurry of a garment salesman trying to con a buyer or a highbrow lecturer trying to dazzle an audience; a deliberate loosening of syntax . . . and a deliberate play with the phrasings of plebeian speech, but often, also, the kind that vibrates with cultural ambition . . .[30]

It is an assimilated language which still derives much of its character and energy from Yiddish. There is, indeed, a close parallel between the Jewish son's pulling out of the first- or second-generation immigrant Jewish family into the material, political, social spaces of America, and the Jewish-American writer's residual use of Yiddish. A story by Cynthia Ozick called 'Envy, Or, Yiddish in America' (1969) shows an enraged, failed Yiddish novelist berating the traitors (such as

Philip Roth) who court fame and success by writing in American:

> *Jewish* novelists! Savages! The allrightnik's children, all they
> know is to curse the allrightnik! Their Yiddish! One word
> here, one word there. *Shikseh* on one page, *putz* on the other,
> and that's the whole vocabulary! And when they give a try at
> phonetic rendition! Darling God![31]

Portnoy, visiting a Gentile family as a boy and feeling the need
to assert his Jewishness, speaks for the novelist: 'Talk Yiddish?
How? I've got twenty-five words to my name – half of them
dirty, and the rest mispronounced' (*PC*, p. 253).

Americanized Portnoy, humiliated and accused of being 'a
self-hating Jew' in Israel, refusing to join in his sister's mourn-
ing for the six million ('it is coming out of my ears already, the
saga of the suffering Jews!' (*PC*, p. 84)), shares his author's
desire to get off the ship and live. Nevertheless, Roth is not free
of the contemporary Jewish-American writer's predicament –
which is still acute, even if traditional Jewishness in America is
becoming 'vestigial'.[32] On one side the predicament leads to the
Jewish writers describing themselves as 'mythical Gentiles',[33]
like Norman Mailer's Sergius O'Shaughnessy in *The Deer Park*
and 'The Time of Her Time'; on the other, to an increasing
concern with Israel, as in Saul Bellow's journal *To Jerusalem
and Back* (1976). Roth's heroes, far from 'letting go' of their
Jewishness, more and more frequently need to set their own
struggles – which, after all, usually consist of nothing more
harrowing than an over-protected childhood, a disastrous
marriage to a Gentile, and a painful course of analysis – in the
context of the history of the Jews.

Tarnopol, like Portnoy, tries to reject his parents' generation's stories of Gentile persecution as 'irrelevant to the kind of
life that I intend to lead' (*MLAM*, p. 53), but one of the key
stories of his childhood for his analyst is that in 1942, aged 9,
when his family moves house, the child goes back to the old
home and thinks the Nazis have come and taken his mother
away. Tarnopol calls this story in his journal 'The Diary of
Anne Frank's Contemporary'. In *The Professor of Desire*

Kepesh's personal endeavours to become a 'marvellous' Kepesh are put in their place first by the visit to Prague and last by the story of his father's old friend, who has survived the concentration camps. In *The Ghost Writer* the theme emerges fully in Nathan's 'useful fiction' about the mysterious, attractive girl who is staying with the Lonoffs. He imagines that she is Anne Frank, who has survived incognito and whom he is going to take home to his family.

> Oh, marry me, Anne Frank, exonerate me before my outraged elders of this idiotic indictment! Heedless of Jewish feeling? Indifferent to Jewish survival? Brutal about their well-being? Who dares to accuse of such unthinking crimes the husband of Anne Frank? (*GW*, p. 148)

Roth's extraordinary achievement here is to have dared to render the idea of Anne Frank's survival as a characteristically 'tasteless' Jewish joke, a comic ploy used to illustrate Nathan's self-absorbed conflict between being a Jewish son and a Jewish writer. At the same time, it is a grave and startling metaphor for the conscience of the Jewish-American novelist, who has not been in the concentration camps, or in hiding, or in exile, who is not in sympathy with the chauvinist militancy of Zionism, and whose writing expresses the longing of Anne Frank's words in her diary: '*the time will come when we are people again, and not just Jews*' (*GW*, p. 124).

3

'BEYOND THE PALE':
AMERICAN REALITY FROM THE
SECOND WORLD WAR TO
WATERGATE

Philip Roth's fiction strains itself to shed the burden of Jewish traditions and proscriptions. But, in breaking out of the hermetic, self-protecting world of orthodox authoritarianism, he finds the world 'out there' to be another kind of comic nightmare. The liberated Jewish conscience, let loose into the disintegration of the American Dream, finds itself deracinated and homeless. American society and politics, by the late sixties, are a grotesque travesty of what the Jewish immigrants had travelled towards: liberty, peace, security, a decent liberal democracy. Roth writes out of an alienation from both claustrophobic Jewishness and vertiginous America. Though the books in which he tackles the condition of America are less richly imagined and less funny than the 'Jewish' novels, the two kinds of writing are vitally related: it is no aberration for Roth to turn immediately from Portnoy's struggle inside the Jewish family to Nixon's corruption of the American language.

The relation between the Jewish 'complaint' and American 'reality' is most sensationally expressed in the long story of 1970, 'On the Air'.[34] Milton Lippman, wartime talent scout, good Jewish husband and father, begins it with a frantic, Portnovian diatribe against 'The Answer Man', star of the *goyische* radio networks ('Someday, you son of a bitch, there will be a program with a Jew on it giving out the answers!'), and a series of humble but inspired letters to Albert Einstein in Princeton. Milton suggests himself as agent for 'The Albert Einstein Show', which will prove to a hostile world that 'THE

45

GENIUS OF ALL TIME IS A JEW!' Einstein's resemblance to Harpo Marx can only be an advantage; and Milton's experience as an agent (teaching two black New Jersey shoe-shine boys to tap dance without saying 'shee-yit' all the time) and his belief in the power of radio ('Hearing is believing!') make him eager to discuss with the great genius the possibility of 'the Famous Albert Einstein talking around a fireside with someone of the caliber of a Tony Martin'.

But Milton and his timid wife and son never reach Princeton. In a succession of short, increasingly bizarre scenes with snappy radio-show titles ('The Lone Ranger', 'Contest Announcement'), the Jewish family sets out on Sunday into brutal, dangerous Gentile America — like Lemuel Pitkin setting out hopefully in Nathanael West's *A Cool Million*, or Karl Rossmann making his way through Kafka's *America* — to find themselves inside a comic proof of Lippman's theory that 'the world is some kind of – of *show*!' The talent scout who has a passion for viewing reality as radio comedy – Hitler, the Pope, Mussolini, Mrs Roosevelt: 'acts that they were giving away for *nothing*!' – becomes the victim of 'a perfect situation comedy! Perfect for his Jewish network!', a black farce of violence, anti-Semitism, cruelty and humiliation.

In 'Scully's Tavern', nothing he sees is explicable:

This was no bullshit tavern from the radio, *this was the real thing* – only more so! The dead decapitated baby deer! Ice picks in the dartboard! and a World War One bayonet! And those women – swollen, brainless, beer-inflated zeppelins! And those little children, pounds of lard (from *eating* lard) in little dark suits and white dresses, clutching to their little sleeping faces the Sunday School books telling them how the Jews killed their Jesus Christ!

Little Lippman hides under his mother's dress, the bartender roars at the Chinamen in the kitchen, eight fat women burst into Kate Smith's popular radio song 'When the Moon Comes Over the Mountain', someone comes out of the back ('A black tumor hung from the end of his hand!') – is it a bowling alley or a radio studio? At 'Howard Johnson's', the friendly 'icecream jerk' who says he is Kate Smith's nephew has a scoop for an arm and turns out to be a mentally defective epileptic. Pop Scully ('the emperor of icecream') offers little Lippman a choice of ink, wood, glass, shoe polish or newspaper-flavoured ice-cream. The boy goes grey when he eats print, and, as he and his mother pass out, 'The Chief' makes his entrance, a screaming, violent, trigger-happy 'homo' who insists on comparing the weight of his balls with a pair of Jewish balls. 'Scoop', the icecream boy, has an epileptic fit while the Chief gets high on rhetoric ('Kill the metaphor! Slaughter the simile! Fuck the fable! . . . I'm being driven literal. Scully!'). As Lippman is poised between shooting or being shot by the Gentile comedy team (but the bullet will bounce off his Jewish nose), a 'special bulletin' brings news of Hitler's decision not to shave off his moustache – all disapproving barbers to be exterminated. 'We return you now to our regular pogrom.' There's a competition for the funniest thing that ever happened ('Is it Hitler? Or . . . the Jews? Describe the incident in five hundred words or less and send it in with the head off your neighborhood grocer!'). And so, until the next episode of 'Milton Lippman, Talent Scout!', goodnight 'to all those out there "Beyond the Pale"'.

For all its unusually strenuous surreal extravagance, 'On the Air' is, typically, occupied with Jewish chauvinism and paranoia, Jewish jokes and comic routines. Lippman will be re-worked as Alvin Pepler, the discredited TV-quiz star of *Zuckerman Unbound*, whose complaints against the Gentile strangle-hold on the media echo Lippman's attack on 'The Answer Man'. But 'On the Air' alters the emphasis by concentrating not on emotions – Lippman and his family are ciphers, like Lemuel Pitkin – but on the strangeness of America. The frantic travesties of American myths like 'law and order' or 'happy family Sundays' in this radio show are no stranger than what is out there 'beyond the pale'. Lippman's description of a talent scout as one who must have an eye for 'the strange' – 'he doesn't make things happen, *he only points them out*!' – is also Roth's description of the novelist in America. By using surreal fantasy (or 'Paranoid Hallucination', as he calls the method of

47

'On the Air'),[35] the novelist tries for 'a kind of passage way from the imaginary that comes to seem real to the real that comes to seem imaginary' (*RMAO*, p. 84). Acting as an intermediary between a reality and a fantasy which are as strange as each other, the novelist begins to feel like an alien. Like Roth's 'wandering' Jewish heroes, like his homeless baseball team in *The Great American Novel* ('In this chapter the fortunate reader who has never felt himself a stranger in his own land, may pick up some idea of what it is like' (*GAN*, p. 145)), the writer in America 'feels that he does not really live in his own country'.[36]

The phrase occurs in a now very well-known essay called 'Writing American Fiction', published by *Commentary* in March 1961 but first given as a lecture at Stanford in 1960. Like Joan Didion writing in *The White Album* (1979), whose monstrous anecdotes of California in the late 1960s are presented as cumulative evidence of the strangeness of America ('Certain of these images did not fit into any narrative I knew'[37]), Roth starts the essay with an account of a mystery murder of two girls in Chicago, whose mother is sent thousands of dollars and 'a whole new kitchen', and whose self-confessed murderer becomes a cult hero.

> And what is the moral of the story? Simply this: that the American writer in the middle of the twentieth century has his hands full in trying to understand, describe, and then make *credible* much of American reality. It stupefies, it sickens, it infuriates, and finally it is even a kind of embarrassment to one's one meager imagination. The actuality is continually outdoing our talents, and the culture tosses up figures almost daily that are the envy of any novelist. (*RMAO*, pp. 109–10)

He continues with an early parody of Nixon, in his 1960 fight against Kennedy: 'as a real public figure, a political fact, my mind balked at taking him in.' 'What can the writer do with so much of the American reality as it is?' Like Norman Mailer, he can choose participation, presenting 'his life as a substitute for his fiction' (*RMAO*, p. 113), or he can withdraw from 'social and political phenomena' into charm and mysticism (Salinger) or into a generalized humanism (Malamud) or into an inordinately bouncy, muscular prose style (Bellow) in celebration of the separate self, cut off from the unfriendly environment.

Roth does not describe his own intentions in the essay, but his work in the 1960s (*Letting Go*, *When She Was Good*, *Portnoy's Complaint*) shows him conscientiously caught between 'out there' ('All actuality is deadly earnest') and 'in here' ('Nothing but *self*! Locked up in *me*!' (*PC*, p. 280)). He writes about individuals in families and marriages; political or social involvement, like Portnoy's job for Mayor Lindsay, is a secondary subject. Roth has said that the rhetoric of domestic oppression used by Lucy Nelson in his Midwest, 'Gentile' novel *When She Was Good* is the equivalent of a political language of coercion (*RMAO*, p. 10). And, before that, some of his 1950s film reviews and articles for *New Republic* and the *Chicago Review* had been occasions for political satire. For instance, in 'Positive Thinking on Pennsylvania Avenue', Eisenhower's bedtime prayers – 'I know, Lord, that I muffed a few and I'm sorry about that. But both the ones we did all right and the ones we muffed I am turning them all over to you'[38] – are parodied. But not until 1970 does Roth's fiction tackle directly what is grotesque, beyond belief – 'beyond the pale' – in American public life, using the only means that seem appropriate to him, burlesque and black comedy. 'On the Air' is the first in a group of works, written between 1970 and 1974, which turn the subversive energies of bad taste outward from the private struggles of the Jewish son or husband to the realities and myths of America. These are *Our Gang* (1971), 'Starring Tricky and His Friends' (1971), *The Great American Novel* (1973), several essays or skits on American politics ('Cambodia: A Modest Proposal' (1970), 'The President Addresses the Nation' (1973), 'Our Castle' (1974), 'Writing and the Powers that Be' (1974)) and *The Breast* (1972). Though this last is the 'odd book out' in its closeness to *Portnoy* and *The Professor of Desire*, it locks the Jewish hero into a 'reality' as bizarre and alien, as 'Kafkaesque', as the America that the other works describe. By the time these works were written, the Vietnam war years had increased the sense of strangeness felt in 1960:

> One even began to use the word 'America' as though it was the name, not of the place where one had been raised and to which one had a strong spiritual attachment, but of a foreign invader that had conquered the country and with whom one refused, to the best of one's strength and ability, to collaborate. Suddenly America had turned into 'them'. . . (*RMAO*, p. 11)

The increase in alienation, the stronger impetus towards political satire, came from one prime source – 'In a word: Nixon' (*RMAO*, p. 45).

Richard Nixon was 'known as a crook in our kitchen', Roth is proud to say, 'some twenty-odd years before this dawned on the majority of Americans as a real possibility' (*RMAO*, p. 10). Roth's family, like many lower-middle-class Jewish Americans, were 'devout New Deal Democrats', passionate supporters of Franklin D. Roosevelt. Some of his relatives even went so far as to vote for Henry Wallace, the Progressive Party candidate in 1948 – 'someone that everybody was calling a Communist', as Mr Kepesh says to his son in *The Professor of Desire*. Roth's father's lifelong liberalism is repeatedly, and affectionately, introduced into the novels: Mr Tarnopol mourns for Roosevelt and Kennedy, Mr Kepesh abominates George Wallace, Mr Zuckerman writes furious anti-war letters to Lyndon Johnson. Roth's wartime childhood was spent in wholehearted patriotic commitment to the American war effort. In college during McCarthy's 'heyday', Roth campaigned for Adlai Stevenson. Post-war patriotism lasted him through Korea until the mid-fifties, when he enlisted in the army (and, like Novotny, was soon discharged with a back injury). But in the 1960s, 'the demythologizing decade' (*RMAO*, p. 81), Roth, like a whole generation of Americans, became disillusioned and alienated. 'What may have been the most propagandized generation of young people in American history', force-fed, silent, straight-laced, suddenly found that 'what was assumed to be beyond reproach became the target of blasphemous assault; what was imagined to be indestructible, impermeable, in the very nature of American things, yielded and collapsed overnight' (*RMAO*, p. 81). The 'Bay of Pigs' crisis, Kennedy's assassination (and then those of Martin Luther King and Bobby Kennedy), Vietnam, Nixon, Chappaquiddick, the destruction of Cambodia and Watergate cumulatively produced a 'countermythology' of desanctification 'to challenge the mythic sense of itself the country had when the decade opened with General Eisenhower, our greatest World War II hero, still presiding' (*RMAO*, p. 82).

Unlike Mailer, Roth has not hurled himself into political action which is then used for literary material. But all his work in the early 1970s is closely related to political events. 'Cambodia: A Modest Proposal' (6 October 1970), which suggests that America should drop the goods of Western civilization on Cambodia – shoes and deep freezes instead of bombs – followed a visit to Cambodia just before the American invasion of April 1970. Parts of *Our Gang* were published from May to September of 1971 (between Calley's My Lai trial in April 1971 and the break-in of Nixon's 'plumbers' to the offices of Ellsberg's psychiatrist in September). Chapters of *The Great American Novel* came out in the spring of 1973, during the early stages of the Watergate trials. 'The President Addresses the Nation', a spoof speech in which Nixon refuses to resign for the good of the country, was published on 14 June 1973, anticipating the real thing by ten months (Nixon's self-defensive statement on 29 April 1974, which was made just over three months before his resignation). 'Our Castle' was published on 19 September 1974, in dismayed response to Ford's pardon of Nixon on 8 September.

In 'Our Castle', Roth compares the position of the American people (as he will compare that of the citizens of Prague) to Kafka's 'Land Surveyor K.' in *The Castle*. Innocent, hopeful, and eager to set to work, K. finds himself 'blocked at every turn by authorities to whose inscrutable edicts and bizarre decrees he is beholden, but whose motives and methods defy his every effort to make sense of them' (*RMAO*, p. 173). The image of thwarted and betrayed innocence explains why Roth returns so

51

often to the age of innocence, the forties and early fifties, and to the two most potent influences in that age's popular culture: radio comedy and baseball. 'On the Air' 'demythologizes' the coziness of the old radio shows, just as *The Great American Novel* demythologizes the game that gave the youthful Portnoy, as 'center fielder for the Seabees', his only full taste of freedom and control. That two of Roth's 1970s burlesques should be set in the 1940s does not imply nostalgic escapism from the 'unreality' of modern America – far from it. The disillusionment of the Second World War generation was most damaging in that it necessitated a revision of childhood.

In his last book, *Zuckerman Unbound*, Roth has Alvin Pepler, speaking in 1969, date the end of American innocence in the late 1950s, with radio having been finally overtaken by television, and the scandal of the rigged TV quiz shows (which Portnoy makes his name investigating) standing for 'the beginning of the end of what's good in this country'.

> 'There is where it began, and where it has ended is with another war again, and one this time that makes you want to scream. And a liar like Nixon as President of the United States. Eisenhower's gift to America. That schmegeggy [a loser, a born failure] in his golf shoes – this is what he leaves for posterity . . . the decline of every decent American thing into liars and lies.' (*ZU*, p. 33)

Alvin, crazed with his complaints, voices the anger and bewilderment of his more rational contemporaries: the whole of their history turns out to have been a 'show' that was rigged.

*

Roth appropriates baseball as a subject for riotous 'demythologizing' not only because he loves and knows it – 'the literature of my boyhood' – or because it embodies the all-American ideals of competitiveness, teamsmanship and toughness ('Winning is the name of the game' (*GAN*, p. 303)), or because (very like whaling) it lends itself, as a major, popular, all-male

American pastime, to the rewriting of 'the great American novel'. He also uses it because Nixon did. The rhetoric of games-playing was one of Nixon's favourite ploys: Nixon would refer to his 'game plan', his 'team players' who would do his 'downfield blocking', and his plans to 'shoot the gap'.[39] Disaffected members of the Nixon regime found this significant. Peter Peterson, sacked as Secretary of Commerce in 1972, said: 'There's only one star. . . . If you try to act like a first-team player and publicize yourself, then you aren't going to make it.'[40] Elliott Richardson, who resigned as Attorney General on 20 October 1973, said: 'His use of football analogies was so revealing . . . anything was OK except what the referee sees and blows the whistle on.'[41] Once Tricky had taken football or baseball as a metaphor for the Vietnam war, those games could not be made clean again: 'Goodbye, Columbus', and goodbye to American innocence. (The 'demythologizing' of the playing fields of Eton on the battlefields of Europe would be an apt historical analogy.) So *Our Gang* and *The Great American Novel* are closely related, though one is a parody of Nixon, his aides and the media, and the other is a farcical epic of a wartime baseball team of cripples, midgets and losers, narrated by Roth's latter-day Ishmael, one 'Wordsmith', a verbose, geriatric ex-sports writer. When Roth was writing *The Great American Novel* he would wear his baseball cap (*RMAO*, p. 102); and when Tricky has an advisory conference in *Our Gang* he dons his football uniform and has his aides dress as coaches. I don't mean that Philip Roth identifies with Nixon, but, as Salman Rushdie has pointed out,[42] referring to his attack on Mrs Gandhi in *Midnight's Children* (1981), there is a parallel between what the novelist and the political despot want to do with a country: repossess it.

Roth was not alone, of course, in finding Nixon hair-raisingly grotesque and in identifying his distortion of the language as the key to what was happening to America. He cites Mencken's satire on President Warren Gamaliel Harding's 'puerile prose style', which Mencken called 'Gamalielese', as one of the inspirations for *Our Gang* (with Orwell's *1984* and 'Politics and the English Language', Chaplin's *The Great*

Dictator, and Abbott and Costello's 'slapstick comedy'). Mencken as a critic of 'American public rhetoric' stands at the head of a long line of American intellectuals who feel themselves to be a subculture, speaking a foreign language in their own country. In satirizing government's dangerous gobbledegook, Roth is in company with, for example, Mary McCarthy, who comments on the inaccuracy of the language used at the trial of Medina (Calley's company commander, court-martialled in August 1971 for the killings at My Lai in 1968, and acquitted in September 1971) and on the feelings of 'innocent non-participation' fostered by terms like 'pacification'.[43] The same point is made by Norman Mailer in *The Armies of the Night*, who gives an example of 'totalitarianese' – 'language which succeeds in stripping itself of any moral content' – in the mouth of a Pentagon spokesman, who defended the violence used against the protest marchers on the Pentagon on October 1967 by saying: 'We feel . . . our action is consistent with objectives of security and control faced with varying levels of dissent.'[44]

Journalists, lawyers and political commentators writing on Watergate commented repeatedly on the way that the sinister distortion of language in the Johnson war years was intensified under Nixon and his people. Johnson's 'sanitizing language of war', as Frank Mankiewicz calls it in *Nixon's Road to Watergate*, words like 'pacification', 're-location', 'defoliation', 'gooks', 'wasting' and 'attrition', developed under Nixon into phrases such as 'limited duration protective reaction strikes' for 'bombing'. 'Doublespeak' was applied not just to the war in Vietnam but to the 'war' against revolutionaries at home: the infiltration of campuses in the early 1970s was dressed up in terms such as 'electronic surveillance', 'mail coverage' and 'development of campus sources' (i.e. buying students as government spies). 'The language became so sanitized that the Nixon people didn't know a lie when they saw one.' 'True' words became unusable once Nixon had described the withdrawal of the American presence in South Vietnam as 'peace with honour'.[45]

Disgust at the opportunist use of such vocabulary is not new:

Hemingway's *Farewell to Arms*, E. E. Cummings's *The Enormous Room* and John Dos Passos's *USA* all made the point, long before, about the First World War. But 'Nixonese' was the nadir, and Watergate, with its revelations of the discontinuity between the private 'expletive deleted' language of the tapes and the public rhetoric, was its climax. Over and over again, people wrote of the unreality of Watergate. Judge Sirica, in an honest, painstaking account of the part he played, wrote of events that, offered as a film scenario, 'would have been laughed out of Hollywood',[46] and of the President's having 'lost his grip on reality'.[47] As an illustration, he gives a characteristic public statement made by Nixon during Watergate: 'I have a quality which is – I guess I must have inherited it from my midwestern mother and father – which is that the tougher it gets the cooler I get.'[48] David Frost, describing his post-Watergate interviews with the discredited Nixon, comments repeatedly on his banal, lengthy evasions, on the random inconsistencies of his arguments, and on his opportunistic responses to factual questions: 'The Nixon strategy' (as when he was President) 'seemed to be to get from one moment to the next.'[49] In the end, only one reaction to the whole of Nixon's career seemed appropriate. Sirica describes it taking place in his courtroom:

> When we were playing the White House tapes, it was not uncommon for someone in the courtroom to break into a sort of perverse laughter as the ugly and damaging details of the cover-up were heard at first hand. I repeatedly had to remind those present that no laughter would be tolerated. . . . Hundley [John Mitchell's lawyer] joked, 'How do you feel about crying, judge?'[50]

The difficulty that this presents for the parodist is precisely the difficulty described by Roth in 'Writing American Fiction': the actuality outdoes the writer's talents. When 'reality' is so far 'beyond the pale' that it can be met only with 'a sort of perverse laughter', the parodist becomes all but redundant. *Our Gang* suffers from this problem. Martin Green calls it 'the least exciting of his books . . . merely a duty done, dues paid by the writer as citizen',[51] and it does seem at once too strenuous and, in retrospect, insufficiently outrageous.

Tricky defends the rights of the unborn in a bid for the 'embryo' vote in the 1972 elections. A 'troubled citizen' asks how he can balance this against the killings at My Lai ('If I should find in the evidence against the lieutenant anything whatsoever that I cannot square with my personal belief in the sanctity of human life, including the life of the yet unborn, I will disqualify myself as a judge and pass the entire matter on to the Vice President' (*OG*, p. 16)). The press asks him his plans for dealing with radical foetuses ('this administration does not intend to sit idly by and do nothing while American women are being kicked in the stomach by a bunch of violent five-month-olds' (*OG*, p. 19)). The Boy Scouts march on the Capitol, accusing him of favouring sexual intercourse. Tricky offers to go on television and say that he is queer. His 'Political Coach', 'the Professor', advises instead a smear campaign to link the revolting Boy Scouts with a defected baseball star, now in Copenhagen. Denmark is invaded, three Boy Scouts are killed, and Tricky demonstrates on television, by slashing up the Bill of Rights and the Ten Commandments with a scout knife, that this apparently inoffensive instrument is a vicious communist torture weapon. He goes into hospital to have his sweat glands removed ('that is how dedicated I am to dissociating myself from anything remotely *resembling* a human body' (*OG*, p. 30)) and is found dead, curled up naked in a foetal position in a plastic baggie full of water. Thousands of people converge on Washington, pleading guilty to the murder; in hell, Tricky starts his campaign to replace the Devil:

And that is why I can assure you, my fellow Fallen, that down here where no holds are barred and nothing is sacred, you are going to see a New Dixon, a Dixon such as I could only dream of being while still an American human being, a Dixon who humbly submits that he has what it takes in experience and energy to be the kind of Devil all you lost souls deserve. (*OG*, p. 137)

The intention of this 'baggy pants burlesque skit' (*RMAO*,

pp. 42–3) is to make the real Nixon no less ludicrous than Tricky Dixon; thus, references to actual events in Nixon's past (the Checkers speech, the Alger Hiss affair, the meeting with Khrushchev, the change of policy over China) are frequent, and the relevance of the Boy Scout débâcle to the Kent State shootings, or the blockade of Denmark to the bombing of Cambodia, is quite obvious. The ironies against Nixon are blatant: Tricky is made to say: 'This is probably just about the most fantastic opportunity for self-aggrandizement I've come upon since [Alger] Hiss' (*OG*, p. 60), or 'Five minutes later I didn't even remember what it was I'd *endorsed*' (*OG*, p. 28), or 'I actually think the American people can be made to believe anything' (*OG*, p. 156). Cunning, subtlety, discretion, are not in order here: Roth wants to express his outrage ('triggered', he says, by Nixon's preferential treatment of Lieutenant Calley) in broad strokes of 'Bad Taste'. Hence the silly names (the late President John F. Charisma, the Western White House at San Dementia, reporters called Mr Asslick or Mr Hardnose), the absurd farcical scenes (Dixon's coaching session in football gear), and the crude caricatures of Agnew or Kissinger or Billy Graham. What rescues all this from being, as Martin Green suggests, merely conscientious, is the linguistic bravado of Roth's parodies not just of 'Nixonese' but of the language of journalists, television reporters and political advisers. Erect Severhead's reports from Washington ('A hushed hush pervades the corridors of power. Great men whisper whispers while a stunned capital awaits' (*OG*, p. 106)), Bilge Secretary Blurb's White House announcements ('I don't know if I want to use a highly inflammatory word like that at a time like this' (*OG*, p. 123)), and other spoofs of what Roth calls 'the platitudinous mentality of the media' and 'the fine art of government lying' (*RMAO*, pp. 50–1) provide the context for an energetic parody of Nixon's public and private speech. Tricky's favourite references (to his Quaker parents, his legal know-how), his habitual turns of phrase ('and I want to make one thing perfectly clear'), his usual targets (the misfits, the bums, the malcontents, anarchy, socialism, welfarism, etc.), his rhetorical practices (games-playing metaphors, slurs by association, moral attitudinizing) are very thoroughly de-bunked. Like *Portnoy, Our Gang* is a book which is a mouth, a narrative working entirely through dislocated voices that speak a language so patently corrupt that it must produce, in those who understand what is being done to the words they also have to use, 'a sort of perverse laughter'.

*

In *The Great American Novel*, Roth allows himself more freedom than in *Our Gang*, and the phrases he uses for it – 'Sheer Playfulness', 'writing for pleasure', 'comic inventive-ness' – insist that here he is really 'letting go'. *The Great American Novel* has baseball as its obsession, but is not limited to a single satirical target, like *Our Gang*. It has a narrator, Wordsmith, but unlike Portnoy or Tarnopol he disappears, Ishmael-fashion, in the middle of the book. Roth is as lavish and minute in his treatment of baseball as Melville in his descrip-tions of whaling, but he incorporates other subjects freely. The writing of *The Great American Novel* emulates the liberation which Roth felt while playing baseball at school, and which he expresses in Portnoy's centre-field ecstasies ('You can't im-agine how truly glorious it is out there, so alone in all that space' (*PC*, p. 76)) and in Roland Agni's eloquence ('When I'm standin' in there, waitin' for the pitch, ya' know, I hold the big end of the bat so straight and so still, ya' can balance a dime on the end of it' (*GAN*, p. 262)).

But, for all its taking of liberties (and it is a calculatedly self-indulgent book), *The Great American Novel* is as pointed a political satire as *Our Gang*, and as much concerned with the corrupting power of rhetoric and the loss of national inno-cence. The mythic words on which Roth's generation was brought up – winning, patriotism, gamesmanship – are desanc-tified; greed, fear, racism and political ambition are disclosed as the motive forces behind the 'all-American ideals', history is seen to be rewritten by the authorities, as in *1984*, and the victims of these conspiracies find themselves (like the American novelist) to be exiles in their own land: 'What the hell good is a country to you anyway, if there is no place in it you can call your own?' (*GAN*, p. 363).

Furious, neglected Wordsmith, once the famous sports writer Smitty, now in Valhalla, a geriatric home, 'archaic in my own century, a humorous relic in my own native land' (*GAN*, pp. 18–19), tells of the journey into oblivion of the Ruppert Mundys. Back in the 1920s this Newark team and its champion centre-fielder, Luke Gofannon, under the management of 'Glorious Mundy', were the heroes of General Oakhart's now forgotten Patriot League. But in the 1930s the team passed into the hands of the cynical Mundy brothers, to whom baseball was a business, not 'a national religion'. Luke Gofannon was sold, a fight to the death was on between the indisciplined young star pitcher, Gil Gamesh, and the old umpire Mike the Mouth, and in 1943 the Ruppert ball park was leased to the government as an embarkation camp, with much highflown rhetoric: 'Yes, what the hallowed playing fields of Eton had been to the British officers of long, long ago, Mundy Park would be to GI Joe of World War Two' (*GAN*, p. 62). The bizarrely assorted Mundys, now at the bottom of the league, were sent out on the road, never to go home again. Apart from Roland Agni, a champion centre-fielder put in the team by his parents as a cure for pride, the Mundys consist of an absent-minded French Canadian (whose speciality was 'dropping high infield flyers'), a 14-year-old boy in search of a nickname, a criminal alcoholic from Nicaragua, a one-legged catcher, a left-fielder who knocks himself out on the wall in every game, a one-armed right-fielder who is traded for a vindictive midget, and various has-beens and oldies whose pitching is greeted with cries of 'What time you say she's due in?' (*GAN*, p. 140). Whether riding in the Patriot League cities' garbage trucks, or playing against the inmates of an insane asylum ('Those fellas ain't thinkin' (*GAN*, p. 186)), or caught up in the fight between the rival midgets, or on an inexplicable winning streak due to the doctoring of their breakfast Wheaties, or being indoctrinated by Gil Gamesh, who returns as a communist double agent, the ignominious picaresque adventures of the Ruppert Mundys are grotesque in the extreme. Those who watch them are 'transfixed . . . by the strangeness of things . . . by all that is beyond the pale and just does not seem to belong in this otherwise cozy and familiar world of ours' (GAN, p. 141).

Roth allows himself a number of loosely linked comic turns – a brothel where the prostitutes play American moms ('I can give you "Rock-a-bye-Baby" for ninety-eight cents, but that's the cheapest we got' (GAN, p. 166)), a disastrous missionary attempt to convert the African natives to American sport ('Mistah Baseball – he dead' (GAN, p. 321)) and the media's sentimental enthusiasm for the midgets. But these incidentals contribute to the farcical discrediting of the 'ailing' national myths which the Ruppert Mundys at once believe in and parody. At the end, the purge of communist elements from General Oakhart's Patriot League, and Smitty's last stand against the Un-American Activities Committee ('I refuse to participate in this lunatic comedy' (GAN, p. 388)), makes it plain that Smitty's 'paranoid fantasy' 'has its origins in something we all recognize as *having taken place*' (RMAO, p. 84). As its title and its first sentence ('Call me Smitty') suggest, *The Great American Novel* is as intent on literary parody as on using baseball as a political metaphor. The American dream of 'winning', on which Smitty is eloquent ('Win hands down, win going away, win by a landslide, win by accident, win by a nose, win without deserving to win – you just can't beat it, however you slice it. Winning is the tops' (GAN, p. 303)) applies as much to the rivalry for the title 'great American novelist' as to the competition between ballplayers, or politicians. Smitty sets the exiled wanderings of the Ruppert Mundys against the alienation of Hester Prynne, or Huck Finn, or Ahab. Some of the novel's best extravagances are its pastiches of Melville and of Hemingway:

'How is he on the light trim?' I asked.

'Not bad for Chicago,' Hem said, giving the barber his due.

'Yes,' I said, 'it is a rough town for a light trim where there are a lot of Polacks.'

'In the National League,' said Hem, 'so is Pittsburgh.'
(GAN, p. 38)

Although the narrative of *The Great American Novel* is committed to anarchy and is, perhaps, too conscientiously in pursuit of irreverence, its political subject, as Roth says, is authority: 'the question of who or what shall have influence and jurisdiction over one's life' (*RMAO*, p. 78). Who is to influence Smitty's prose, and what is to destroy the Ruppert Mundys, are related matters. As in all Roth's work, the question of authority is at once a literary, a political and a personal question.

4

'YOU MUST CHANGE YOUR LIFE': MENTORS, DOUBLES AND LITERARY INFLUENCES IN THE SEARCH FOR SELF

Political coercion and obstruction are public versions of family, marital and psychological struggles. The question of who or what shall have influence over the self applies to every area of Roth's work, and quite as much to narrative modes as to subject-matter. I have already said that his novels describe various forms of opposition between discipline and freedom, and it is already apparent that in his treatment of this opposition Roth is highly literary, referential and self-conscious. Moreover, each of his books explicitly relates the predicament of his characters to the writer's narrative choices and solutions. And so his spokesmen are frequently writers or teachers of literature, as self-conscious as their author about the influence of books on their lives. 'Literature got me into this', says Tarnopol, 'and literature is gonna have to get me out' (*MLAM*, p. 198).

This explicit relationship between influence in life and in literature is clearly but awkwardly embodied in *When She Was Good* (1967), a long, miserable 'American tragedy' of a girl in a small Midwest town in the 1950s, Lucy Nelson, who despises and all but destroys her liberal, over-protective grandfather, her alcoholic father, her helplessly feminine mother, and the nice but stupid boy who gets her pregnant at the age of 18. Lucy's savage insistence on duty ('You have to do what's *right*' (*WSWG*, p. 175)), her conviction that everyone is at fault except herself, her rage at the smalltown life which traps her, end in frantic self-destruction. Though this is his only novel with a Gentile and provincial setting, and with a woman at its centre, Roth insists on its relation to his other work. Lucy's thwarted bids for freedom are, he says, another version of Portnoy's (*RMAO*, pp. 24, 26), and her coercive rhetoric is like the American government's in the war with Vietnam (*RMAO*, p. 10). Even so, it is the most uncharacteristic and uninspired of his books, doggedly naturalistic, and vacillating uneasily between presenting Lucy as pitiful victim and portraying her as tyrannical monster. The parallel, though, between the restrictions imposed on and enforced by Lucy, and the restrictions Roth places on himself in writing this novel, is a typical one. Roth is trying to write the big, Gentile, American naturalist novel in the tradition of Wolfe, Dreiser or Sinclair Lewis:

> 'Town' meant Iron City, where the logs were brought to be milled and the ore to be dumped into boxcars, the clanging, buzzing, swarming, dusty frontier town to which he walked each schoolday – or in winter, when he went off in a raw morning dimness, ran – through woods aswarm with bear and wolf. So at the sight of Liberty Center, its quiet beauty, its serene order, its gentle summery calm, all that had been held in check in him, all that tenderness of heart that had been for eighteen years his secret burden, even at times his shame, came streaming forth. (*WSWG*, p. 9)

The uncomfortable syntax, the embarrassing archaisms ('aswarm', 'streaming forth'), the dull choice of words ('swarming', 'summery', 'serene'), reveal the straitjacketed writer. This is a mode that suits Roth no better than Lucy's family, town and marriage suit her.

Lucy Nelson does not admit to her literary mentors. She is never to be found reading *Main Street*, or *An American Tragedy*, or *You Can't Go Home Again*. (In fact she reads 'Ozymandias', useful for its image of the desolation wreaked by a 'sneer of cold command'.) Elsewhere, Roth allows himself to be more playful and explicit with 'the question of influence'. At the beginning of *Letting Go*, Gabe Wallach and Libby Herz have a long conversation about James's *The Portrait of a Lady* ('That book . . . is really full of people pushing and pulling at each other' (*LG*, p. 10)), which alerts us to specifically 'Jamesian' traits in the characters – Libby's romantic aspirations, Gabe's 'hanging fire' – and, more generally, to the crucial subject of self-defining choices, crucial not just for *Letting Go* but for all Roth's work. If you are what you have chosen to be, then you must live with it – like Isabel Archer at the end of *The Portrait of a Lady*. But that moral, Jamesian desire of Roth's characters to come to terms with their chosen selves is balked by impenetrable obstacles which owe more to Kafka than to James. What Roth calls 'a deeply vexing sense of characterological enslavement' (*RMAO*, p. 98) – Portnoy's complaint, and that of all the Kepeshes and Zuckermans – is almost always described in literary as well as psychoanalytical terms. In his comments on *My Life as a Man*, Roth refers to the scene in *The Trial*, where K., in the cathedral, hopes that the priest will come down from his pulpit and point him to 'a mode of living completely outside the jurisdiction of the Court'.[52] As Roth sees it, the man in the pulpit is oneself, and the court 'is of one's own devising': the only possible existence, in the world according to Kafka, is an ironic toleration of that trap. Roth's novels describe different versions of 'characterological enslavement' either accepted or resisted, and each version invokes one, or several, literary authorities for the predicament.

When Roth turns David Kepesh, professor of literature, into a breast (*The Breast*, 1972), he makes literary influence into an explicit part of Kepesh's 'enslavement': 'I got it from fiction,' the professor tells his analyst. 'The books I've been teaching – they put the idea in my head. . . . Teaching Gogol and Kafka every year – teaching "The Nose" and "Metamorphosis"' (*PRR*, p. 470). 'I have out-Kafkaed Kafka' (*PRR*, p. 480). But Dr Klinger is there to tell him that 'hormones are hormones and art is art', to make him accept himself as *real*. (It is usual for Roth's psychoanalysts to oppose or belittle their patients' *literary* analyses of their problems.) Kepesh's task is to accept that 'It is only life, and I am only human.'

For him there is no way out of the monstrous situation, not even through literary interpretation. There is only the unrelenting education in his own misfortune. What he learns by the end is that, whatever else it is, it is the real thing: he *is* a breast, and must act accordingly. (*RMAO*, p. 63)

Kepesh's last words, addressed to 'my fellow mammalians', are a quotation from Rilke ('You must change your life'). In this extreme parable of 'characterological enslavement' Kepesh has progressed from literary explanations, fantasies, frustration and disbelief, to an acceptance of his grotesque self, an acceptance he finds it easiest to express, however, in a quotation.

Kepesh in *The Breast* succeeds where Portnoy leaves off and where Tarnopol fails. The writer and teacher in *My Life as a Man* is compelled to explain his breakdown through a series of fictions that make his life into texts for interpretation. The more his fictional Zuckerman protests that he is 'real', not a character out of *The Trial*, the less Tarnopol finds it possible to accept that 'this is me who is me being me and none other' (*MLAM*, p. 337). He cannot write himself out of his predicament. Tarnopol's self-conscious blockage makes for a frantically energetic, garrulous, funny novel – Roth's equivalent to Bellow's *Herzog* – which is (necessarily) repetitive and self-indulgent. More shapely and assured versions of literary influence as an explicit part of 'characterological enslavement' are found in *The Professor of Desire* and *The Ghost Writer*.

The Professor of Desire (1977) is a realist – as opposed to surreal – portrait of David Kepesh (written five years after *The Breast*) which makes elegant, complex use of Chekhov and Kafka as authorities for Kepesh's predicament while he is still living 'as a man'. Kepesh is torn between reckless erotic ambitions and conscientious intellectual dedication. Peripheral characters line up from childhood onwards as 'secret sharers' of his two selves: first, his anxious hotelier parents and the vulgar comedian Herbert Bratasky; then the two Swedish girls he lives with in London (while writing his thesis on Arthurian legends), the affectionate Elizabeth and the debauched Birgitta; later, his responsible, chivalrous department head 'Arthur' Schonbrunn and the libidinous poet Baumgarten. His marriage to the sexy, sloppy Helen Baird makes the conflict unmanageable: erotic pleasures are driven out by the professor's need for responsible order; the result is anxiety and impotence. His mother's death seems a judgement on his inability to sustain 'steady, dedicated living' (*PD*, p. 125). The commonsensical Dr Klinger tries to close the gap between libido and conscience, but the real, if temporary, cure comes from Claire Ovington, who is erotic, innocent, virtuous and orderly all in one, and brings Kepesh a period of simple peace and satisfaction.

He celebrates by returning to his abandoned book on Chekhov, whose stories tenderly express the 'humiliations and failures' of 'socialized beings' who 'seek a way out of the shell of restrictions and convention' (*PD*, p. 124). At the end of the novel, Claire and Kepesh are visited in the country by Kepesh's widowed father and the father's old friend, who, having survived the concentration camps, says that his ambition had always been to be 'a human being . . . someone that could see and understand how we lived, and what was real' (*PD*, p. 201). Even though his sufferings have been so much less, Kepesh feels himself to be failing in that ambition. Sensing by now that his passion for Claire is an 'interim', not a solution, he tells her that the comical, pathetic visit of the two old men is like a Chekhov story, and that they two are left (like the lovers at the end of 'The Lady with the Little Dog') knowing 'that the most complicated and difficult part was only just beginning' (*PD*, p. 203).

In Chekhov's 'The Duel', the story that is central to Kepesh's work on that author, the 'weaseling, slovenly, intelligent, literary-minded seducer' Layevsky, imprisoned by what an analyst would call 'the libidinous fallacy', finds his antagonist and 'secret sharer' in the rationalist zoologist Von Koren, who believes that the race should be improved by exterminating 'lepers' like Layevsky. Von Koren almost kills him in their duel in the Caucasus, but is distracted by the intervention of a man of faith. The duel releases 'a sense of shame and sinfulness' in Layevsky; he makes an honest woman of his mistress and tries to 'change his life'. Von Koren, who is leaving, apologizes to the reformed Layevsky for having misjudged him: 'Nobody knows the real truth,' he says. As Von Koren's boat disappears into a dark, stormy Black Sea, Layevsky reflects:

In the search for truth man makes two steps forward and one step back. Suffering, mistakes, and weariness in life thrust them back, but the thirst for truth and stubborn will drive them on and on. And who knows? Perhaps they will reach the real truth at last.[53]

Kepesh too is making two steps forward and one step back. But his acceptance of the limits to personal happiness in an unhappy world is only partly allowed to take its tone from the dignity and pathos of 'a muted Chekhov tale of ordinary human affliction' (PD, p. 204). Before this last scene, Roth boldly externalizes the professor's 'blockage' by sending Kepesh and Claire to Prague. Here, of course, Kafka is the spiritual authority. Kepesh discusses Kafka's relevance to the citizens of Prague with a Czech professor, who, sacked from his post, ironically tolerates his fate by translating Moby Dick, painstakingly and pointlessly, into Czech. The Jewish-American and the Czech teachers of literature salute each other's blockages, the one sexual, the other political, in terms that exactly describe what Roth's novels do with literary influence – batten on to it, consume it, use and abuse it, and finally break free of it to find their own voice and style:

> 'Well,' he says, putting a hand on my arm in a kind and fatherly way, 'to each obstructed citizen his own Kafka.'
> 'And to each angry man his own Melville,' I reply. 'But then what are bookish people to do with all the great prose they read –'
> '– but sink their teeth into it. Exactly. Into the books, instead of into the hand that throttles them.' (PD, p. 137)

Kepesh and Claire visit Kafka's grave, and find it next to the graves of all those who perished in the camps. In a café, sitting next to two alluring prostitutes, he writes his next lecture (couched in the form of Kafka's 'Report to an Academy'), which sets out honestly to explain the relevance of his own libidinous history to his teaching of literature. His own desires, the professor's 'life as a man', must be acknowledged in the classroom (he will tell his students) if they are to understand how *Madame Bovary* and other great novels 'concerned with erotic desire' have any 'referential' relationship to the students' own lives and to the life of their teacher. Like Kafka's ape speaking to the Academy, the professor wishes to give to his students 'an open account of the life I formerly led as a human being. I am devoted to fiction, and I assure you that in time I will tell you whatever I may know about it, but in truth nothing lives in me like my life' (*PD*, pp. 144, 147). But at night he dreams of being taken (by Herbert Bratasky) to visit Kafka's whore, a decrepit old woman who offers to show him her withered cunt in the cause of scholarship. The desecration of Kafka's image in the dream violently subverts the lecture's attempt to reconcile the conscientious, dedicated life of the mind with the shameful, secret life of the body. The four Prague episodes – the professor, the cemetery, the lecture, the dream – are not explained; characteristically, they are left to jostle and overlap uncomfortably in the reader's mind. The total effect is to set Professor Kepesh in the mortifying, inexplicable, blocked world of Kafka (or Gogol) rather than the dignified, tender Chekhovian world.

But, after all, the professor is not a citizen of Prague; his relatives left Europe and were not killed in the camps; he can teach, write and speak freely (even if America in the 1970s does seem unreal and alien). What obstructs him is an internal conflict. Kafka, as Kepesh tells Claire, says to his sausage-eating colleague that 'the only fit food for a man is half a lemon' (*PD*, p. 141); by contrast, the lemon in the professor's fridge is replaced by his caring mother's packets of frozen food. The visit to Prague is weighted with guilt. Martin Green describes the sources of that guilt well, in his comments on Roth's essay 'Looking at Kafka' (1973). This extraordinary essay completes a study of Kafka by imagining that he has survived and come to America and is, in 1942, the 9-year-old Roth's Hebrew schoolteacher, invited home by the family to be matched with Aunt Rhoda:

> The contrast . . . is between the self-denying and self-defeating Czech, spiritual athlete and ascetic, and the brash

and greedy son of immigrants, the Jew who got away, whose writings embody the all-voracious culture around him, even as they bitterly criticize it.[54]

In his own professional life, Roth's editing of the Penguin 'Writers from the Other Europe' series could be seen as an expiation of that guilt. His admiration for writers who died in the war (Bruno Schulz, the brilliant Galician author of two novels, who translated *The Trial* into Polish, and was shot by an SS agent in 1942), or who endured the camps (Tadeusz Borowski, who survived Auschwitz and Dachau and killed himself in Warsaw in 1951), or who are living under severe prohibitions in Czechoslovakia (Milan Kundera, to whom *The Ghost Writer* is dedicated, for whose *Laughable Loves* Roth wrote an introduction, and who has also written on Kafka), or whose work has been savagely attacked by the authorities (Danilo Kiš, a Yugoslav writer for whom Bruno Schulz is 'a god'[55]), inevitably involves self-comparisons:

> I am wholly in awe of writers like Sinyavsky and Daniel, of their personal bravery and their uncompromising devotion and dedication to literature. To write in secrecy, to publish pseudonymously, to work in fear of the labor camp, to be despised, ridiculed, and insulted by the mass of writers turning out just what they're supposed to – it would be presumptuous to imagine one's *art* surviving in such a hostile environment, let alone coming through with the dignity and self-possession displayed by Sinyavsky and Daniel at their trial. (*RMAO*, p. 49)[56]

In Kepesh or Zuckerman, Roth projects a complicated attitude, not simply the Jewish-American writer's guilt for the sufferings of eastern European writers and, before that, for the Jews in Europe, but, with it, a kind of wistfulness, even envy, for the writer who has had more to sink his teeth into than books and relationships. This half-shaming sense lurks behind Kepesh's fixation on Kafka and, more comically, behind Nathan's fantasy of Anne Frank's survival in *The Ghost Writer*.

*

Of all Roth's novels, *The Ghost Writer* is the most concentratedly about influence. It is an elegant, small-scale *Bildungsroman*, a 'rite of confirmation', in which the 23-year-old Nathan Zuckerman comes to manhood and dedicates himself to the writer's task in one night spent at the house of the reclusive Russian-Jewish novelist, E. I. Lonoff, deep in the snowy Berkshires. The novel, or rather novella, eschews the straggling, garrulous form of *My Life as a Man* or the loosely linked episodes of *The Professor of Desire* in favour of a coolly controlled structure. Nathan's evening, night and morning at the house encircle two life stories, one real (Nathan's) and one fictive. The 'fictive' story imagines the possibility of the survival of Anne Frank (a play about whose life and death, drawn from her diary, is running on Broadway). Nathan, curious about the position in the household of a mysterious, attractive fellow guest, Amy Bellette (adopted orphan? mistress? family friend? amanuensis?), identifies her as Anne Frank – an Anne Frank who had, after all, survived the camps. The two stories, his and hers, are carefully opposed: the Jewish son who angers his own loving parents by 'betraying' the Jews in the story he has written ('Higher Education') is set against the legendary, 'sainted' Jewish daughter, whom he imagines sacrificing a post-war reunion with her father in order that, through her assumed death, her art may live. Just as she has survived to see her diary immortalize the sufferings of the Jews in Europe, and now claims kinship not with her real father but with the writer Lonoff, recorder of the 'exclusion and confinement' of the race, so Nathan needs to turn to a writer-father. At first we take Anne Frank's story as literal; only gradually does it appear that it is a 'useful fiction', Nathan's fantasy (comparable to Kepesh's dream of Kafka's whore in *The Professor of Desire*). Through this invention Nathan acts out his own anxiety about the double burden placed on the Jewish writer: disinheritance from those he must write about, responsibility to their history.

All the other parallels in this book are as carefully balanced as that between Nathan and Amy – those between the Jewish-American writers, the self-denying Lonoff and the self-publicizing Abranavel; between wife and girl in Lonoff's house, the martyred Hope and the sensual Amy; between highpowered New York and country life in the Berkshires, an old landscape of the American Transcendentalists, where the writer is thrown on his own resources; between Nathan's real father and his literary father, Lonoff. The two references pinned up in Lonoff's study (where Nathan eavesdrops, masturbates, writes to his father, inspects Lonoff's library and sleeps in the day-bed), one of them to Chopin and Byron ('tenderness, boldness, love and contempt' (*GW*, p. 68)) and the other to Henry James (restraint, renunciation, the high road of art), sum up the alternatives. The choice, as always in Roth, but most neatly diagrammed here, is between the 'hunger artist's' asceticism and anxiety, and the 'hungry panther's' appetite for full absorption in the world of sex, love and power. Can the artist have both, or must he deny himself? Lonoff's index card refers the aspiring Nathan to Henry James's story 'The Middle Years', in which a young doctor sacrifices a fortune in order to minister to the dying novelist Dencombe, a perfectionist and compulsive corrector of his own work (like Lonoff, and James) who is aware that he has just missed greatness, and whose last words bleakly describe the artist's fate: 'We work in the dark – we do what we can – we give what we have. Our doubt is our passion and our passion is our task. The rest is the madness of art' (*GW*, p. 102). James's austere ideal of dedication is the model for Lonoff's asceticism, which his disciple has admired in the stories of 'thwarted, secretive, imprisoned souls' (*GW*, p. 15) and which he now sees in Lonoff's life: 'a man, his destiny, and his work – all one' (*GW*, p. 67). The stories are 'visions of terminal restraint'; the characters (always 'a bachelor, a widower, an orphan, a foundling, or a reluctant fiancé') are blocked in their smallest impulses towards self-surrender by those 'devoted underlings' of 'Sanity, Responsibility and Self-Respect', 'the timetable, the rainstorm, the headache, the busy signal, the traffic jam, and, most loyal of all, the last-minute doubt' (*GW*, p. 17). The small details of Lonoff's behaviour, closely observed by Nathan – his fussiness over the fire and the record-player, his annotation of magazine articles, the half an egg he wants for breakfast – are symptomatic of the restraint that prevents him from wanting to do anything except 'turn sentences around', least of all run off to Italy (always an idealized escape route for Roth's heroes) with the mysterious Amy. The ageing maestro renounces the temptations of young love as he has renounced those of fame, while his wife, driven berserk (a brilliantly painful comic study) by living for thirty-five years with so much 'moral fibre', tries to abdicate in favour of her rival: 'You get the creative writer – and I get to go!' (*GW*, p. 151).

While love and despair rage around him, Lonoff (like the Czech professor) is 'kind and fatherly', if ironical, to his disciple. But Nathan has not yet chosen Lonovian, or Jamesian, completeness: there is a gap, pointed out by both his fathers, between what he writes and what he is. And Lonoff has not been his only model; earlier he had met and admired Felix Abranavel, wryly summed up by Lonoff:

> 'Beautiful wives, beautiful mistresses, alimony the size of the national debt, polar expeditions, war-front reportage, famous friends, famous enemies, breakdowns, public lectures, five-hundred-page novels every third year, and still . . . time and energy left over for all that self-absorption. . . . Like him? No. But impressed, oh yes. Absolutely. It's no picnic up there in the egosphere.' (*GW*, p. 49)

Lonoff and Abranavel, possible models for the aspiring Jewish-American writer, suggest composite models: Nathan compares Lonoff to Singer; his pilgrimage invokes Charlie Citrine's to Humboldt in Bellow's *Humboldt's Gift*, and Abranavel has more than a touch of Mailer. But Philip Roth is also projected, as the young beginner before *Goodbye, Columbus*, as the much-courted and famous author of *Portnoy*, as the established and private man of letters. In his 'middle years', he is ghost-writing himself as disciple and as master, so that his subject, in this grave, marvellously controlled comic novel, is at once the illusions and the deprivations of a literary vocation.

*

'Nathan Dedalus's' choosing of a new father prompts him to tell his life story to Lonoff, who is described at the end as 'the picture of the chief rabbi, the archdeacon, the magisterial high priest of perpetual sorrows.' The need for an 'archdeacon' to whom the son or writer can confess, and who will tell him how to change his life, is common to Roth's characters. They fix on writers or analysts rather than on priests or rabbis, but, like K. in the cathedral, they want instruction and consolation. The novels, in their pursuit of 'who or what shall have influence over the self', are full of magus figures. They may be literary sages, 'singing masters' of the soul, like James or Kafka. They may be treacherous coaches like Tricky, or spokesmen for repressive authoritarianism, like Rabbi Binder or Judge Wapter – or Lucy Nelson. They may be cherishing but oppressive fathers, or destructively over-possessive wives or mothers. They may be 'secret sharers' (the term, from Conrad, used by Kepesh for Baumgarten and by Nathan for Alvin Pepler) who seem, however grotesquely, to enact a suppressed part of the blocked self. Or the 'blocked' hero may himself be a teacher, a mentor to others, whose courses, like Tarnopol's on 'transgression and punishment' or Kepesh's on desire, express their obsessions. Most of the mentors and *alter egos* are, as in Kafka, ominous rather than reassuring. They inspire the kind of distrust that is the basis of *Our Gang*, or the fear that is a running joke in *Zuckerman Unbound* (1981).

After the success of his novel *Carnovsky* in 1969 (the year of *Portnoy*, of course), people accost Nathan Zuckerman (thirteen years older now than he was in *The Ghost Writer*) on buses and in the street, write him abusive letters, spill out their fantasies to his answering service, report his invented affairs in the gossip columns, and take his name in vain on television. Whether he eats a snack in a café or takes a famous actress out to dinner, he is public property, and needs an armed chauffeur. Having tried to enfranchise himself by writing *Carnovsky*, he finds himself imprisoned by Fame. Reality – 'le vrai', as Flaubert calls it – is taking its revenge. New York seems to consist entirely of his would-be assassins or confiding fans. Alvin Pepler, the disgruntled, loquacious scapegoat of the TV quiz scandals of the 1950s, dogs Nathan's steps, with marvellous comic insistence, his manic adulation rapidly turning to abuse, as though summoned up by Nathan's paranoia: 'This Peplerian barrage is what? Zeitgeist overspill? Newark poltergeist? Tribal retribution? Secret Sharer? P. as my pop self? . . . He who's made fantasy of others now fantasy of others' (*ZU*, p. 159).

It is tempting to ridicule *Zuckerman Unbound*, as some critics did, for protesting too much about the painful problems of wealth and fame, though Nathan's fear of assassination in New York can strike no one as exaggerated. But, even if this novel, for all its comic brio, is self-regarding, it fits exactly into the pattern of Roth's work. Comical Nathan, the complaining self who goes in fear of his *Doppelgänger*, is also the disinherited son. In a brilliant family scene round the father's deathbed, Nathan, having tried to offer consolation with a brand-new scientific theory of the endlessly self-renewing life of the universe, hears the word 'bastard' painstakingly pronounced: it is his father's last word. Later, his brother tells him what had caused his father's death: reading *Carnovsky*. 'You killed him, Nathan, with that book. *Of course* he said "Bastard". He'd seen it! . . . You don't believe me, do you? You can't believe that what you write about people has *real consequences*' (*ZU*, pp. 217–18). The book ends as Nathan is driven by his armed chauffeur through the Newark streets of his childhood, now a ghetto. 'Who are you supposed to be?' the black occupant of what was his father's house asks him. '"No one," replied Zuckerman, and that was the end of that' (*ZU*, p. 224).

Like Portnoy, Nathan is locked inside himself, unamused by the joke ('you keep ducking when you should be smiling'), desperate for advice. His agent has his case in hand ('My concern is defusing the persecution mania, Nathan' (*ZU*, p. 129)), but it is a matter of Nathan's dislocation from 'le vrai' that, in this novel so tightly contained within the New York literary world, the literary agent should have taken over the role of analyst.

*

Part of the originality of *Portnoy's Complaint* was its use of the analysand's monologue as a literary stratagem. It is not, though, a novel about analysis. Dr Spielvogel is silent until his punchline, and Portnoy's confession is, as Roth says, 'highly stylized'. Nor does Portnoy change his life: part of his complaint is that 'his sense of himself . . . is so *fixed*' (*RMAO*, p. 89). And, of course, the analyst cannot simply tell the patient to 'change his life'; his version of the patient may be rejected, the blockage may be impenetrable. Of all the magus figures in Roth, the analysts are the least authoritarian.

Roth uses them first as escape routes for unhappy young married women. In a story of 1963 called 'The Psychoanalytic Special'[57] a suburban housewife hooked on clandestine affairs, who 'desperately' wants 'to be changed', commutes four times a week to tell Dr Spielvogel about her dreams, her boring marriage and her departed lover. In the end she finds that being cured is worse than the affliction. Libby, in *Letting Go*, pays a weeping visit which she can't afford to a Dr Lumin, to tell him that Paul neglects her, that she loves Gabe, and that she feels cracked. Dr Lumin is matter-of-fact: 'These are real problems. . . . But what's this cracked business? How far does it get us?' (*LG*, p. 351).

These disheartening forays into analysis lead on to the silent reappearance of Dr Spielvogel in *Portnoy* as the reader's 'secret sharer'. After *Portnoy*, analysis becomes a central, active ingredient in the comical blockages of Tarnopol and Kepesh. Spielvogel's adage – 'tolerate it' – helps Tarnopol, in *My Life as a Man*, to save himself from Maureen, but his rejection of the analyst's 'reductivism' ('Does your wife remind you of your mother?') culminates in a furious sense of betrayal when he finds that Spielvogel has, himself, 'written him up'. The analyst has published his patient's case history (with certain significant features altered) in an article called 'Creativity: The Narcissism of the Artist', a use of himself as 'evidence' which that very narcissism renders Tarnopol quite unable to excuse. Kepesh in *The Professor of Desire* is irritated by Dr Klinger's dogged 'demythologizing' of his case. Only Kepesh as a breast begins to respond to the 'demystifying' of his predicament. 'You are not insane,' Klinger tells the breast. 'It *is* something that has happened to you . . . *this is no delusion*' (*PRR*, p. 471). This is the only treatment that Roth's analysts can provide: the best they can do is to make people tolerate their condition, however surreal it may seem to them, as *real* – and thus their condition may become tolerable. Such 'demythologizing' is liable to be funny: Roth's scenes of analysis often take the form of comic routines, two-handers between the funny man and his stooge (roles that may alternate between patient and analyst):

'Your sperm? What about your sperm?'
'My semen – I leave it places.'
'Yes?'
'I smear it places. I go to people's houses and I leave it – places.'
'You break into people's houses?'
'No, no,' I said sharply – what did he think I was, a madman? 'I'm invited. I go to the bathroom. I leave it somewhere . . .'
. . . 'Speak up, please,' said the doctor.
'I sealed an envelope with it,' I said in a loud voice. 'My bill to the telephone company.'
Again Spielvogel smiled. 'Now that is an original touch, Mr Tarnopol.'
And again I broke into sobs. 'What does it mean!'
'Come now,' said Dr Spielvogel, 'what do you think it "means"? . . .'
'That I'm completely out of control!' I said, sobbing. 'That I don't know what I'm doing any more!'
'That you're angry,' he said, slapping the arm of his chair. 'That you are furious. You are not *out* of control – you are *under* control. Maureen's control. You spurt the anger everywhere, except where it belongs. There you spurt tears.'
(*MLAM*, pp. 215–16)

Maureen Tarnopol is in analysis too, but her pain is not made available to us. In Tarnopol's 'life as her man' she is the monstrous 'lunatic' who traps him into marrying her by faking a pregnancy test, sabotages his professional life, goes through

76

abortions and suicide attempts before her violent death, and leaves Tarnopol unmanned and obsessed. Of all Roth's female characters, Maureen is the most frantic and destructive. That she has her own story to tell is frequently suggested (not least by the book's epigram, taken from her diary: 'I could be his Muse, if only he'd let me'). But she is seen, in the main, as the 'unmanning' influence on Tarnopol, and thus takes her place among the pantheon of obstructors, authorities or mentors who encompass Roth's complaining heroes. He makes some early, conscientious attempts to engage with the psychology of women such as Libby and Martha in *Letting Go* or Lucy Nelson in *When She Was Good*, but the later women characters are placed in either obstructive or enfranchising relations to the son/husband/writer/complainant. They stand, in the main, as Dionysian or daemonic influences opposed to the Apollonian reason and wisdom of the male analysts and writers. Only rarely is female sexuality apprehended without guilt or dread, and then it is usually felt as consolation, something to hold on to after a bad dream:

> I awaken perspiring. . . . Then, blessedly, I find Claire, a big warm animal of my own species, my very own mate of the other gender, and encircling her with my arms – drawing her sheer creatureliness up against the length of my body – I begin to recall [the dream]. (*PD*, p. 148)

Roth's male characters overlap with each other and with Roth; his women characters can be grouped together as over-protective mothers, or as monstrously unmanning wives, or as consoling, tender, sensible girlfriends, or as recklessly libidinous sexual objects. Occasionally, like Portnoy's 'Monkey' – dressed for Mayor Lindsay's dinner like a stripper, murmuring obscenities down the Assistant Commissioner's phone, understanding 'Leda and the Swan' with her cunt – they burst through the confines of their type with a kind of vengeful comic energy. And in the last two novels there are developments: Hope Lonoff of *The Ghost Writer* and Caesara O'Shea, the ironical film star of *Zuckerman Unbound*, are unexpected and exactly seen.

Nevertheless, Roth's use of women characters as part of an examination of 'who or what shall have authority over the (male) self' does not endear him to feminist critics. Alix Kates Shulman, for example, is dissatisfied with *When She Was Good*, which, she says, like other 'male-oriented' versions of the American forties and fifties such as *Summer of '42* and *The Last Picture Show*, 'neglects' the female point of view.[58] (A feminist antidote to the novel would be Lisa Alther's *Kinflicks*.) Sarah Cohen dislikes 'Philip Roth's Would-Be Patriarchs and their *Shikses* and Shrews'.[59] Roth is impatient with the 'Feminist Right', as he makes clear in his review of Alan Lelchuk's *American Mischief*, which, he says, will be called sexist 'for demonstrating . . . that there are indeed women in America as broken and resentful as the women in America are coming to proclaim themselves to be' (*RMAO*, p. 176). If Roth's fiction does demean women, it can only be seen to do so paradoxically. The greediest male dreams of sexual power and gratification are felt by a man who has been turned into a breast and is completely humiliated and helpless. That literal enactment of 'breast envy' is the most extreme of Roth's subservient male fantasies; his men are vulnerable, envious and afraid of women, not domineering chauvinists. Portnoy is really no exception: his insistence that well-brought-up girls should suck him off is only skin-deep bravado. Accusations of chauvinism might be more accurately directed against the thinness with which these girls are characterized in Portnoy's narrative.

But this is ultimately more a question of fictional methods than of sexual politics. I called *Zuckerman Unbound* a self-regarding novel, because it seems to treat Roth's early fame rather solemnly. But it is a tautological criticism, since Roth's novels are *about* self-regard, and their difficulty lies in reconciling 'le vrai' with the narcissistic quest for self. The mentors – literary, spiritual, sexual – who are posted around Roth's complainants are there because they play some part in the struggle towards an acceptance of

> the unalterable necessity
> of being this unalterable animal.

(The lines are from Wallace Stevens's 'Aesthétique du Mal', quoted at the start of *Letting Go*.) Rendered 'unfit', like Novotny, by some undiagnosable pain, the butt of some inexplicable joke, making complaints and appeals in all directions but essentially on their own, Roth's Kafkaesque buffoons totter towards a way of feeling *real*, of saying 'this is me who is me being me and none other'. Most of the books end (like Bellow's *Herzog*) as this process begins: no one is allowed to finish. The parallel, as Zuckerman tries to explain to his dying father, is with the universe, which, according to the big-bang theory, is 'being reborn and reborn and reborn, without end'

5

FINISHING

The brilliance and energy of Roth's fiction results from an idiosyncratic, successful negotiation between 'in here' and 'out there'. The apparent ease with which he closes that gap disguises a difficulty fundamental to the modern writer: the outside world seems a bizarre joke; the individual is locked inside his own dismay and frustration. But, if the frantic, exhaustive complaints of Roth's 'blocked' Jewish heroes were entirely masturbatory and solipsistic, his fiction would limit itself at the expense of coming to terms with the outside world. *Portnoy's Complaint* succeeds as a comic extravaganza as well as a howl of pain because the 'complaint' takes its life throughout from the autonomous, odd, insistent realities of 'le vrai'. A longer book on Philip Roth would be able to give space to his precise, comic acuity, the hardness of his outlines, what Alfred Kazin calls his worrying of 'surprising details and odd facts in people's behaviour'.[60] The Patimkin family, Gabe Wallach's academic colleagues, the JP with gout who marries Paul and Libby, Tarnopol's taxi driver ('I said to him, "You're Samuel Beckett, man!" And you know what he said? He says, "No, I'm Vladimir Nabokov"' (*MLAM*, p. 323)), Mr and Mrs Portnoy, Hope Lonoff hurling her wine glass at the wall ('She can glue it'), the New York literary scene, Nathan's answering service ('It could just be a pervert, Mr Zuckerman, I wouldn't worry'), the Madison Avenue funeral parlour outside his window, the family gathering round his father's deathbed: all such solid occasions show a relish for 'the nature of things as they are'[61] which rescues his material from being submerged by the process of self-analysis.

What gives Roth's fiction its character is the welding of such exact 'external' realities into narratives of an inner voice, whose 'plots' are confessions, traumas, fantasies and complaints. The apparently easy negotiation between self and world is an extremely cunning structural achievement. Roth's characteristic voice – exclamatory, intimate, conversational, moving rapidly between the vulgar and the literary – disguises the organization of his fiction with its appearance of free flow. In *Portnoy's Complaint*, especially, there is an inextricable relationship between 'process' and 'material', voice and narrative, which gives the novel an air of unplotted spontaneity. As Roth says of Kafka's story 'The Burrow', 'no distinction is possible between character and predicament' (*RMAO*, p. 232). But, even if 'the method is the subject',[62] *Portnoy* does have a concealed structure, which gradually moves Alex on (and back, and on again) from childhood case history to adult traumas. While the 'complaint' repeats and returns on itself in the form of the obsessed patient's outpourings, the evidence is being accumulated in groups of anecdotes, loosely strung together as in a stand-up comic's monologue. Other novels use different stratagems (the alternative versions of Tarnopol ironically juxtaposed in *My Life as a Man*, the fluid chronological scheme of *The Professor of Desire*, the one night's visit that holds together *The Ghost Writer*) which give a sense of freedom while maintaining order.

The effect of free flow is a difficult one to sustain. *Letting Go*, *My Life as a Man* and even *Portnoy's Complaint* are, I think, too long, even for their protagonists' dilemmas, which do require over-stretched and over-loaded narratives. In his last two 'Zuckerman variations',[63] Roth has reverted to the length of 'Goodbye, Columbus', a form that Henry James famously called 'the beautiful and blest *nouvelle*'. *The Ghost Writer* was first published in *The New Yorker*, and Roth has worked towards most of his novels by publishing sections which are then revised and incorporated into the final version. (That such work in progress should have found a place in magazines as different as *Esquire* and *The New Yorker* shows that Roth is received as both a 'popular' and as a 'highbrow' writer.) The elegance and control of his last two novels, and Roth's admiration for the long short stories of Chekhov ('The Duel'), Kafka ('The Burrow') and Henry James ('The Middle Years'), suggest that the novella is his ideal form, and that his longer fictions are, essentially, extended short stories.

But the difference between the long, fragmentary, garrulous structure of, for instance, *My Life as a Man* and the tightly restrained form of *The Ghost Writer* is part of the antithesis I have been describing in all of Roth. He is a writer of remarkable virtuosity and adventurousness. The delicate, muted symbolism of an early story like 'The Conversion of the Jews'; the rapid surrealist energies of 'On the Air'; the flat, sombre realism of *When She Was Good*; Wordsmith's gargantuan parodic play in *The Great American Novel*; the penetrating, sympathetic exactness of 'Looking at Kafka', and the reserved, humorous narrative of *The Ghost Writer*: these examples point to an exceptional range. Such a range is not, though, a random variousness of a 'try anything once' kind. As Roth has said, his work describes a deliberate 'zig-zag' (*RMAO*, p. 84). The conscientious, scrupulous early work (*Goodbye, Columbus*, *Letting Go*, *When She Was Good*) is subverted by the 'unbound' tastelessness of *Portnoy's Complaint*; and this countering process is continued. *My Life as a Man* (1974), though certainly a comedy, is also a painful, private antidote to the public high jinks of *The Great American Novel* (1973); *The Professor of Desire* (1977) is a restrained, realist alternative to the surreal version of David Kepesh in *The Breast* (1972); *Zuckerman Unbound* (1981) is a light counterpart to *The Ghost Writer* (1979). The zigzag process is incorporated into and remarked on in *My Life as a Man*, where Tarnopol's two 'Useful Fictions', 'Salad Days' and 'Courting Disaster' (both published separately first by Roth as short stories), are described as written under the influence of, respectively, the id and the superego: the one 'playful', 'naughty', 'perverse', the other feeling and conscientious. The stylistic antithesis between high seriousness and vaudeville knockabout is summed

82

up in Roth's last novel by a working title and subtitle which the novelist Zuckerman (as fond of titles, subtitles and epigrams as the novelist Roth) writes down in his tidy composition book. He remembers a story about Flaubert coming out of his study and seeing his cousin playing with her children. Flaubert says: 'Ils sont dans le vrai.' Zuckerman notes down 'Dans Le Vrai' as a possible title for a novel, then writes beneath it 'Or, How I Made a Fiasco of Fame and Fortune in My Spare Time' (*ZU*, p. 132).

But if Zuckerman is annotating, there, the Rothian 'zigzag', he is also another manifestation of the typical Rothian hero. This individual is attempting to break through some prevention or blockage, to 'crash through the wall' into a free, full sense of self. He is a middle-class urban Jewish-American son, writer and teacher, whose blockage usually takes the form of an over-protected, guilt-inducing childhood, a violently destructive marriage or love affair with a Gentile girl (possibly from a different class) and an attempt to change his life or 'tolerate' his predicament, through analysis and through a series of consolatory relationships. The breakdown – or breakthrough – of this Rothian character is analogous to the violently disillusioning 'crashing through' of America from the innocent, propagandized fifties to the demythologized, surreal seventies.

Philip Roth quotes Delmore Schwartz saying wryly: 'Literary criticism is often very inneresting.' With this dry warning in mind, I am aware of having left out a great deal. Much more might be written about the urban landscape of Roth's novels, and the temporary escape his characters make (like Nathanael West's Miss Lonelyhearts or Bellow's Herzog) from the cities to rural retreats like the Quahsay colony of writers or the Berkshire hills. More could be said about the difficult balance they try to maintain between their professional and secret lives, more about their marital histories, and much more about Roth's language: its mimetic brilliance, extravagant insistence, and ability to be at once brash and thoughtful. Portnoy's relentless jokes and howls of execration are only one of Roth's voices. Example after example might be given of a manner at once lyrical and wry, which projects, through the comic ex-postulations and confessions of the speakers, a knowing, humane authority. I shall finish with three such phrases, one minutely observant, one suavely Jamesian and ironic, and one elegiac: Portnoy's 'fibers of pink lox lodged like sour dental floss in the gaps between my teeth' (*PC*, p. 276); Abranavel's charm 'like a moat so oceanic that you could not even see the great turreted and buttressed thing it had been dug to protect' (*GW*, p. 53); and Zuckerman's falling silent before his father's death (*ZU*, p. 192): 'Enough for now of what is and isn't so. Enough science, enough art, enough of fathers and sons.'

NOTES

1 The point is made by Maurice Charney in *Sexual Fiction* (London: Methuen, 1981), pp. 124ff., who pairs *Portnoy's Complaint* and Erica Jong's *Fear of Flying* as Jewish autobiographical searches for fulfilment.

2 The basis for Portnoy's 'complaint' is Freud's essay of 1912, first translated as 'The Most Prevalent Form of Degradation in Erotic Life' (*Pelican Freud Library*, vol. 7: *On Sexuality*, trans. James Strachey and Angela Richards (Harmondsworth: Penguin, 1977), pp. 245–60). Freud is also the source for the parallel between masturbation and constipation: 'The retention of the faecal mass, which is . . . carried out intentionally by the child to begin with, in order to serve, as it were, as a masturbatory stimulus upon the anal zone or to be employed in his relation to the people looking after him, is also one of the roots of the constipation which is so common among neuropaths' (ibid., ch. 2, 'Infantile Sexuality', p. 104).

3 Tony Tanner, *City of Words: A Study of American Fiction in the Mid Twentieth Century* (London: Cape, 1976), pp. 18–19, 296, 299.

4 Collected in *Wedding Preparations in the Country and Other Stories*, trans. Willa and Edwin Muir, Penguin Modern Classics (Harmondsworth: Penguin, 1978).

5 Herman Melville, *Moby Dick* (1851), ch. 36.

6 Philip Rahv, 'Palefaces and Redskins', *Image and Idea* (1949; rev. 1957); reprinted in *American Critical Essays: 20th Century*, ed. Harold Beaver, World's Classics (London: Oxford University Press, 1959).

7 'Philip Roth: Should Sane Women Shy Away from him at Parties?' (interview with Ronald Hayman), *Sunday Times Magazine*, 22 March 1981, pp. 38–42.

8 Leslie Fiedler, *Waiting for the End* (London: Cape, 1965; Harmondsworth: Pelican, 1967), p. 74.

9 Allen Guttmann, *The Jewish Writer in America* (London: Oxford University Press, 1971), p. 76; Tanner, op. cit., p. 314.

10 Robert L. White, *Forum*, 4 (Winter 1963), pp. 16–22.

11 Bonnie Lyons, *Studies in American Jewish Literature*, 5, 2 (1979), pp. 8–10. Alfred Kazin, in *Bright Book of Life* (1971; London: Secker & Warburg, 1974), cites Updike's Bech as the character who typifies 'the Jew as contemporary American novelist'.

12 Jeremy Larner, 'The Conversion of the Jews', *Partisan Review*, 27 (Fall 1970), p. 761.

13 Dan Yergin, 'Portnoy: A Critical Diagnosis', *Granta* (May Week 1969); quoted in Tanner, op. cit., p. 315.

14 'Jewishness as the novelist's material . . . is constructed folklore.' Kazin, op. cit., p. 138.

15 Leslie Fiedler, 'Cross the Border – Close That Gap: Post-Modernism', *Sphere History of Literature*, vol. 9: *American Literature since 1900*, ed. Marcus Cunliffe (London: Sphere, 1975), p. 359.

16 Roth, 'The Contest for Aaron Gold', *Epoch*, 7–8 (Fall 1955), pp. 37–50.

17 Roth, 'The Day It Snowed', *Chicago Review*, 8 (Fall 1954), p. 36.

18 See Judith Paterson Jones and Guinevera A. Nance, *Philip Roth* (New York: Frederick Ungar, 1981), p. 6, for a reference by Roth in conversation to Flannery O'Connor.

19 Richard Cohen, 'Best Novel – Worst Award', *Congress Bi-Weekly*, 27 (19 December 1960), pp. 12–14.

20 Leslie Fiedler, 'Goodbye, Columbus', *Midstream*, 5 (Summer 1959), pp. 96–9.

21 Fiedler, *Waiting for the End*, p. 104.

22 Philip Roth, 'On The Great American Novel' (1973), *RMAO*, p. 78.

23 Saul Bellow, *Herzog* (1964; Harmondsworth: Penguin, 1965), p. 100.

24 Sigmund Freud, *Jokes and Their Relation to the Unconscious* (1905), trans. James Strachey and Angela Richards, *Pelican Freud Library*, vol. 6 (Harmondsworth: Penguin, 1976), pp. 156–60.

25 Fiedler, *Waiting for the End*, p. 94.

26 Saul Bellow, quoted in *Jewish-American Stories*, ed. Irving Howe, New American Library (New York: Mentor, 1977), p. 11.

27 Saul Bellow, *The Adventures of Augie March* (1953; Harmondsworth: Penguin, 1966), pp. 616–17.

28 Stanley Elkin, *Alex and the Gipsy* (1973; Harmondsworth: Penguin, 1977), p. 13.

29 Stanley Elkin, 'Criers and Kibitzers, Kibitzers and Criers' (1961), in *Jewish-American Stories*, p. 342.

30 Irving Howe, Introduction, *Jewish-American Stories*, p. 15.

31 Cynthia Ozick, 'Envy, Or, Yiddish in America' (1969), in *Jewish-American Stories*, p. 161.

32 Leslie Fiedler describes Roth and his peers as creators of Jews who must be 'if not terminal Jews, at least penultimate ones' (*Waiting for the End*, p. 99), and the Jewish novelist Herbert Gold said in 1961: 'Chicken soup and Yiddish jokes may tarry for a while. But the history of the Jews from now on will be one with the history of everybody else' ('Jewishness and the Younger Intellectuals', *Commentary*, 31 (April 1961), pp. 322–3; quoted in Guttmann, op. cit., p. 10).

33 Fiedler, *Waiting for the End*, p. 108.

34 All quotations from 'On the Air' are from *New American Review*, 10 (August 1970), pp. 7–49.

35 *Our Gang*, 'Watergate Edition' (London: Bantam Books, 1973), p. 222.

36 Roth compares his feelings with Edmund Wilson's and Benjamin DeMott's ('Writing American Fiction', *RMAO*, p. 121). Others who shared them were Joyce Carol Oates (see Raymond Olderman, *Beyond the Waste Land* (New Haven, Conn.: Yale University Press, 1973), p. 4) and Joan Didion (see *The White Album* (1979)).

37 Joan Didion, *The White Album* (Harmondsworth: Penguin, 1979), p. 13.

38 Roth, 'Positive Thinking on Pennsylvania Avenue', *Chicago Review*, 11 (Spring 1957), pp. 21–4.

39 Frank Mankiewicz, *Nixon's Road to Watergate* (London: Hutchinson, 1973), p. 118.

40 Theodore H. White, *Breach of Faith: The Fall of Richard Nixon* (London: Cape, 1975), p. 178.

41 Ibid., p. 180.

42 Salman Rushdie, *A Tall Story* (Arena, BBC2, 8 December 1981).

43 Mary McCarthy, *Medina* (London: Wildwood House, 1973), p. 84.

44 Norman Mailer, *The Armies of the Night* (London: Weidenfeld, 1968), p. 284.

45 Mankiewicz, op. cit., pp. 116, 168, 118, 120.

46 John J. Sirica, *To Set the Record Straight* (New York: Norton, 1979), p. 134.

47 Ibid., p. 167.

48 Ibid., p. 186.

49 David Frost, *I Gave Them a Sword* (London: Macmillan, 1978), p. 185.

50 Sirica, op. cit., p. 259.

51 Green, op. cit., p. xviii.

52 *RMAO*, p. 108; Franz Kafka, *The Trial* (1925), ch. 9, trans. Willa and Edwin Muir (Harmondsworth: Penguin, 1953).

53 Chekhov, 'The Duel', *Select Tales of Chekhov*, vol. 2, trans. Constance Garnett (London: Chatto & Windus, 1962), p. 158.

54 Green, op. cit., p. xi.

55 John Updike, Introduction, Bruno Schulz, *Sanatorium under the Sign of the Hourglass*, Penguin 'Writers from the Other Europe' (1979; repr. London: Picador, 1980), p. ix.

56 Andrei Sinyavsky, author of *The Makepeace Experiment*, and Yuri Daniel, were sentenced in Moscow to seven- and five-year sentences in 1966 for slandering the state. *On Trial*, edited by Max Hayward, was a transcript of their trial, to which Roth refers in this paragraph.

57 Roth, 'The Psychoanalytic Special', *Esquire*, 60 (November 1963), pp. 106 ff.

58 Alix Kates Shulman, 'The War in the Back Seat', *Atlantic*, 230 (July 1972), pp. 50–5.

59 Sarah Cohen, 'Philip Roth's Would-Be Patriarchs and their *Shikses* and Shrews', *Studies in American-Jewish Literature*, 1, 1 (1975), pp. 16–22.

60 Alfred Kazin, op. cit., p. 145.

61 Wallace Stevens, 'The Man with the Blue Guitar'.

62 Howard Junker, 'Will This Finally be Philip Roth's Year?', *New York Magazine*, 13 January 1969; quoted in Tanner, op. cit., p. 316.

63 *MLAM*, p. 115. Tarnopol's sister asks: 'Are you planning to continue to write Zuckerman variations until you have constructed a kind of full-length fictional fugue?'

BIBLIOGRAPHY

WORKS BY PHILIP ROTH

Fiction (book publication)

Goodbye, Columbus. Boston: Houghton Mifflin, 1959. London: Deutsch, 1959. London: Corgi, 1964.

Letting Go. New York: Random House, 1962. London: Deutsch, 1962. London: Corgi, 1964.

When She Was Good. New York: Random House, 1967. London: Cape, 1967. Harmondsworth: Penguin, 1971.

Portnoy's Complaint. New York: Random House, 1969. London: Cape, 1969. London: Corgi, 1971.

Our Gang. New York, Random House, 1971. London: Cape, 1971. 'Watergate Edition', London: Bantam Books, 1973.

The Breast. New York: Holt, Rinehart & Winston, 1972. London: Cape, 1973. London: Corgi, 1974. Revised 1980 for *A Philip Roth Reader*. London: Cape, 1980.

The Great American Novel. New York: Holt, Rinehart & Winston, 1973. London: Cape, 1973. Harmondsworth: Penguin, 1981.

My Life as a Man. New York: Holt, Rinehart & Winston, 1974. London: Cape, 1974. London: Corgi, 1976.

The Professor of Desire. New York: Farrar, Straus & Giroux, 1977. London: Cape, 1978. London: Corgi, 1978.

The Ghost Writer. New York: Farrar, Straus & Giroux, 1979. London: Cape, 1979. Harmondsworth: Penguin, 1980.

Zuckerman Unbound. New York: Farrar, Straus & Giroux, 1981. London: Cape, 1981.

Stories

This list does not include early versions and sections of Roth's novels published in magazines.

'Philosophy, Or Something Like That'. *Et Cetera* (May 1952), pp. 5, 16.

'The Box of Truths'. *Et Cetera* (October 1952), pp. 10–12.

'The Fence'. *Et Cetera* (May 1953), pp. 18–23.

'Armando and the Frauds'. *Et Cetera* (October 1953), pp. 21–32.

'The Final Delivery of Mr Thorn'. *Et Cetera* (May 1954), pp. 20–8.

'The Day It Snowed'. *Chicago Review*, 8 (Fall 1954), pp. 34–45.

'The Contest for Aaron Gold'. *Epoch*, 5–6 (Fall 1955), pp. 37–51.

'You Can't Tell a Man by the Song he Sings'. *Commentary*, 24 (November 1957), pp. 445–50. Reprinted in *GC*.

'The Conversion of the Jews'. *Paris Review*, 18 (Spring 1958), pp. 24–40. Reprinted in *GC*.

'Epstein'. *Paris Review*, 19 (Summer 1958), pp. 13–36. Reprinted in *GC*.

'Heard Melodies Are Sweeter'. *Esquire*, 50 (August 1958), p. 58.

'Expect the Vandals'. *Esquire*, 50 (December 1958), pp. 208–28.

'Goodbye, Columbus'. *Paris Review*, 20 (Autumn–Winter 1958–9), pp. 71–179. Reprinted in *GC*.

'Defender of the Faith'. *New Yorker*, 35 (14 March 1959), pp. 44–50. Reprinted in *GC*.

'Eli, the Fanatic'. *Commentary*, 27 (April 1959), pp. 292–309. Reprinted in *GC*.

'The Love Vessel'. *Dial*, 1, 1 (Fall 1959), pp. 41–68.

'Good Girl'. *Cosmopolitan*, 148 (May 1960), pp. 98–103.

'The Mistaken'. *American Judaism*, 10 (Fall 1960), p. 10.

'Novotny's Pain'. *New Yorker*, 27 October 1962, pp. 45–56. Revised and reprinted in *PRR*.

'Psychoanalytic Special'. *Esquire*, 60 (November 1963), p. 106.

'On the Air'. *New American Review*, 10 (August 1970), pp. 7–49.

Collections

Reading Myself and Others. New York: Farrar, Straus & Giroux, 1975. London: Cape, 1975. London: Corgi, 1978. Contains:

'Writing and the Powers That Be'. *La Trappola e la Nudità: Lo Scrittore e il Potere*, ed. Walter Mauro and Elena Clementelli (Milan: Rizzoli, 1974); in English, in *The American Poetry Review* (July/August 1974).

'On *Portnoy's Complaint*'. *The New York Times Book Review*, 23 February 1969.

'Document Dated July 27, 1969'. An unmailed letter from Philip Roth to Diana Trilling.

'How Did You Come To Write That Book, Anyway?' *The American Poetry Review* (July/August 1974).

'On *Our Gang*'. *The Atlantic Monthly* (December 1971); reprinted as

an afterword to the 'Watergate Edition' of *OG* as 'On Satirizing Nixon'.

'The President Addresses the Nation'. *The New York Review of Books*, 14 June 1973; also included, abridged, in *Watergate Capers*, Yale Drama School, performed November/December 1973.

'On *The Breast*'. *The New York Review of Books*, 19 October 1972.

'On *The Great American Novel*'. *Partisan Review*, 3 (1973).

'On *My Life as a Man*'. *The Literary Guild* (June 1974).

'After Eight Books'. *The Ontario Review*, 1 (Fall 1974).

'Writing American Fiction'. *Commentary* (March 1961).

'Some New Jewish Stereotypes'. *American Judaism* (Winter 1961).

'Writing About Jews'. *Commentary* (December 1963).

'The Story of Three Stories'. *The New York Times*, 24 October 1971.

'The Newark Public Library'. *The New York Times*, 1 March 1969.

'My Baseball Years'. *The New York Times*, 2 April 1973.

'Cambodia: A Modest Proposal'. *Look*, 6 October 1970.

'Our Castle'. *The Village Voice*, 19 September 1974.

'Imagining the Erotic: Three Introductions': 'Alan Lelchuk', *Esquire* (October 1972); 'Milan Kundera', portions in *Esquire* (March 1974) and in *The American Poetry Review* (March/April 1974), reprinted and revised as introduction to *Laughable Loves* (New York: Knopf, 1974; Harmondsworth: Penguin, 1975); 'Fredrica Wagman', introduction to *Playing House, ou les jeux réprouvés* (Paris: Seghers, 1974).

'Imagining Jews'. *The New York Review of Books*, 29 September 1974.

'I Always Wanted You to Admire My Fasting, or, Looking At Kafka'. *American Review*, 17 May 1973.

A Philip Roth Reader. New York: Farrar, Straus & Giroux, 1980. London: Cape, 1980. Contains:

Extracts from: *My Life As A Man*, *The Ghost Writer*, *The Professor of Desire*, *Our Gang*, *The Great American Novel*, *Portnoy's Complaint*, *Letting Go*, *When She Was Good*.

'I Always Wanted You to Admire My Fasting, or, Looking at Kafka'. In *RMAO*.

'Tricky's Farewell Speech'. Reissue of 'The President Addresses the Nation'. In *RMAO*.

'Novotny's Pain'. *The New Yorker*, 27 October 1962, pp. 45–56; revised 1980.

The Breast. 1972; revised 1980.

Adaptations of Philip Roth's Works

'Eli, the Fanatic'. Adapted by Irv Bauer for Broadway, 1964.

Unlikely Heroes. Three stories from *Goodbye, Columbus* ('Defender of the Faith', 'Epstein', 'Eli, the Fanatic'), adapted by Larry Arrick for Broadway, 1971.

Goodbye, Columbus. Film, directed by Larry Peerce. Paramount, USA, 1969.

Portnoy's Complaint. Film, directed by Ernest Lehman. Columbia-Warner, USA, 1972.

The Watergate Follies. 'The President Addresses the Nation' adapted for Yale Repertory Theater production, 1973.

Editions by Philip Roth

General editor, 'Writers from the Other Europe' series. Harmondsworth: Penguin. Includes:

Andrzejewski, Jerzy. *Ashes and Diamonds*. Introduction by Heinrich Böll. Harmondsworth: Penguin, 1980.

Borowski, Tadeusz. *This Way for the Gas, Ladies and Gentlemen*. Introduction by Jan Kott. Harmondsworth: Penguin, 1976.

Kiš, Danilo. *A Tomb for Boris Davidovich*. Introduction by Joseph Brodsky. Harmondsworth: Penguin, 1980.

Kundera, Milan. *The Farewell Party*. Introduction by Elizabeth Pochoda. Harmondsworth: Penguin, 1977.

—— *Laughable Loves*. Introduction by Philip Roth, first printed in *Esquire* (April 1974); reprinted in *RMAO*. Harmondsworth: Penguin, 1975.

Schulz, Bruno. *Sanatorium under the Sign of the Hourglass*. Introduction by John Updike. Harmondsworth: Penguin, 1979. Repr. London: Pan Books/Picador, 1980.

—— *The Street of Crocodiles*. Introduction by Jerzy Ficowski. Harmondsworth: Penguin, 1977. Repr. London: Pan Books/Picador, 1980.

BIBLIOGRAPHY

A full list of reviews and essays by and about Roth up to 1973 appears in Bernard F. Rodgers, Jr, *Philip Roth: A Bibliography*. Scarecrow Author Bibliographies, No. 19. Metuchen, NJ: Scarecrow Press, 1974.

SELECTED CRITICISM OF PHILIP ROTH

Books

Jones, J. P., and Nance, G. A. *Philip Roth*. New York: Ungar, 1981.

Meeter, Glenn. *Philip Roth and Bernard Malamud: A Critical Essay*. Grand Rapids, Mich.: William B. Eerdmans, 1968.

Pinsker, Sanford. *The Comedy That 'Hoits': An Essay on the Fiction*

of Philip Roth. Columbia, Mo.: University of Missouri Press, 1975.

Rodgers, Bernard F., Jr. *Philip Roth.* Boston: Twayne, 1978.

Articles or books containing sections on Roth

Allen, Mary. 'Philip Roth: When She Was Good She Was Horrid'. *The Necessary Blankness: Women in Major American Fiction of the Sixties*, pp. 70–96. Urbana, Ill.: University of Illinois Press, 1976.

Alter, Robert. 'When He Is Bad'. *Commentary*, 44 (November 1967), p. 86.

—— 'The Education of David Kepesh'. *Partisan Review*, 46 (1979), pp. 478–81.

Bellow, Saul. 'The Swamp of Prosperity'. Review of *Goodbye, Columbus. Commentary*, 28 (July 1959), p. 77.

—— 'Some Notes on Recent American Fiction'. In Marcus Klein (ed.), *The American Novel Since World War II.* Greenwich, Conn.: Fawcett World Publications, 1969.

Bettelheim, Bruno. 'Portnoy Psychoanalyzed'. *Midstream*, 15 (June–July 1969), pp. 3–10.

Charney, Maurice. 'Sexuality and Self-Fulfilment: *Portnoy's Complaint* and *Fear of Flying'. Sexual Fiction*, pp. 113–31. London: Methuen, 1981.

Cohen, Richard. 'Best Novel – Worst Award'. *Congress Bi-Weekly*, 27 (19 December 1960), pp. 12–14.

Cohen, Sarah. 'Philip Roth's Would-Be Patriarchs and their *Shikses* and Shrews'. *Studies in American Jewish Literature*, 1, 1 (1975), pp. 16–22.

Crews, Frederick. 'Uplift'. *New York Review of Books*, 16 November 1972, pp. 18–20.

Deer, Irving and Harriet. 'Philip Roth and the Crisis in American Fiction'. *Minnesota Review*, 6, 4 (1966), pp. 353–60.

Detweiler, Robert. 'Philip Roth and the Test of the Dialogic Life'. *Four Spiritual Crises in Mid-Century American Fiction*, pp. 25–35. University of Florida Monographs, No. 14. Gainesville, Fla: University of Florida, 1963.

Drabble, Margaret. 'Clean Breast'. *The Listener*, 89 (22 March 1973), pp. 37–8.

Epstein, Joseph. 'Saul Bellow of Chicago'. *The New York Times Book Review*, 9 May 1971, p. 4.

Fiedler, Leslie A. *Waiting for the End.* New York: Stein & Day, 1964. London: Cape, 1965. Harmondsworth: Penguin, 1967.

—— 'The Image of Newark and the Indignities of Love: Notes on Philip Roth'. Review of *Goodbye, Columbus. Midstream*, 5 (Summer 1959), pp. 96–9.

—— 'Cross the Border – Close that Gap: Post-Modernism'. *Sphere History of Literature.* Vol. 9: Marcus Cunliffe (ed.), *American*

Literature since 1900, pp. 344–66. London: Sphere, 1975.

Friedman, Alan Warren. 'The Jew's Complaint in Recent American Fiction: Beyond Exodus and still in the Wilderness'. *Southern Review*, 8 (1972), pp. 41–59.

Gass, William. 'The Sporting News'. *The New York Review of Books*, 31 May 1973, p. 7.

Geismar, Maxwell. 'The American Short Story Today'. *Studies on the Left*, 4 (Spring 1964), pp. 21–7.

Green, Martin. Introduction, *A Philip Roth Reader*. New York: Farrar, Straus & Giroux, 1980. London: Cape, 1980.

Gross, John. 'Marjorie Morningstar, PhD'. *New Statesman*, 64 (30 November 1962), p. 784.

—— 'Falsie'. *New Statesman*, 85 (23 March 1973), p. 430.

Guttmann, Allen. *The Jewish Writer in America*. London: Oxford University Press, 1971.

Hayman, Ronald. 'Philip Roth: Should Sane Women Shy Away from him at Parties?' Interview with Roth, *Sunday Times Magazine*, 22 March 1981, pp. 38–42.

Hicks, Granville. 'Literary Horizons'. *Saturday Review*, 22 February 1969, pp. 38–9.

Hoffman, F. J. *The Modern Novel in America*. Chicago, Ill.: Regnery, 1963.

Howe, Irving. 'The Suburbs of Babylon'. *New Republic*, 15 June 1959, p. 17.

—— 'Philip Roth Reconsidered'. *Commentary*, 54 (December 1972), pp. 69–77. Reprinted in *The Critical Point*. New York: Delta, 1973.

Junker, Howard. 'Will This Finally Be Philip Roth's Year?' *New York Magazine*, 13 January 1969.

Kazin, Alfred. 'The Vanity of Human Wishes'. *Reporter*, 27 (16 August 1962), p. 54.

—— 'The Earthly City of the Jews'. *Bright Book of Life* (1971, 1973). London: Secker & Warburg, 1974.

Larner, Jeremy. 'The Conversion of the Jews'. *Partisan Review*, 27 (Fall 1970), p. 761.

Leonard, John. 'Fathers and Ghosts'. *The New York Review of Books*, 25 October 1979, p. 4.

Lyons, Bonnie. 'Bellowmalamudroth and the American Jewish Genre – Alive and Well'. *Studies in American Jewish Literature*, 5, 2 (1979), pp. 8–10.

McDaniel, John N. *The Fiction of Philip Roth*. Haddonfield, NJ: Haddonfield House, 1974.

Malin, Irving. *Jews and Americans*. Carbondale, Ill.: Southern Illinois University Press, 1965.

—— (ed.). *Contemporary American Jewish Literature*. Bloomington, Ind.: Indiana University Press, 1973.

Olderman, Raymond M. *Beyond the Waste Land: The American Novel in the Nineteen-Sixties*. New Haven, Conn., and London: Yale University Press, 1972.

Pinsker, Sanford. 'Reading Philip Roth Reading Philip Roth'. *Studies in American Jewish Literature*, 3, 2 (1977–8), pp. 14–18.

Podhoretz, Norman. 'The Gloom of Philip Roth' (1962). Repr. *Doings and Undoings*, pp. 236–43. London: Hart-Davis, 1965.

Prescott, Peter S. 'Roth in Full Flower'. *Newsweek*, 10 September 1979, pp. 72–3.

Raban, Jonathan. *The Technique of Modern Fiction*. Notre Dame, Ind.: Indiana University Press, 1968.

—— 'The New Philip Roth'. *Novel*, 2 (Winter 1969), pp. 153–63.

Rubin, Stephen E. 'Dialog: Philip Roth'. *Chicago Tribune Magazine*, 25 September 1977, pp. 74–5.

Schechner, Mark. 'Philip Roth', *Partisan Review* (Fall 1974), pp. 410–27.

Shulman, Alix Kates. 'The War in the Back Seat'. *Atlantic*, 230 (July 1972), pp. 50–5.

Siegel, Ben. 'The Myths of Summer: Philip Roth's *The Great American Novel*'. *Contemporary Literature*, 17 (Spring 1976), pp. 171–90.

Soloratoff, Theodore. 'Philip Roth and the Jewish Moralists'. *Chicago Review*, 13 (Winter 1959), pp. 87–99.

—— 'The Journey of Philip Roth'. *Atlantic*, 223 (April 1969), pp. 64–72.

—— 'Fiction'. *Esquire* (October 1972), pp. 82–4.

Tanner, Tony. 'Fictionalized Recall – or "The Settling of Scores! The Pursuit of Dreams!"' *City of Words: American Fiction 1950–1970*, pp. 295–321. New York: Harper & Row, 1971. London: Cape, 1971. Paperback edn, London: Cape, 1976.

Theroux, Paul. Review of *Our Gang*. *The Listener*, 86 (25 November 1971), p. 733.

Wall, Stephen. 'Come the Revolution'. *The Observer* (12 November 1967), p. 28.

Weinberg, Helen. *The New Novel in America: The Kafkan Mode in Contemporary Fiction*. Minneapolis, Minn.: University of Minnesota Press, 1966.

White, Robert L. 'The English Instructor as Hero: Two Novels by Roth and Malamud'. *Forum*, 4 (Winter 1963), pp. 16–22.

Wisse, Ruth. 'Requiem in Several Voices'. *The Schlemiel as Modern Hero*, pp. 118–23. Chicago, Ill.: University of Chicago Press, 1971.

Wolff, Geoffrey. 'Beyond Portnoy'. *Newsweek* (3 August 1970), pp. 66–77.

Yergin, Dan. 'Portnoy: A Critical Diagnosis'. *Granta* (May Week 1969).